THE ADLARD COLES BOOK OF

Electronic Navigation

TIM BARTLETT

ARD COLES NAUTICAL
LONDON

Published by Adlard Coles Nautical
an imprint of A & C Black (Publishers) Ltd
37 Soho Square, London W1D 3QZ
www.adlardcoles.com

Copyright © Tim Bartlett 2005

First edition 2005

ISBN 0-7136-5715-4
ISBN 978-0-7136-5715-9

A CIP catalogue record for this book is available
from the British Library.

A & C Black uses paper produced with
elemental chlorine-free pulp, harvested from
managed sustainable forests.

Typeset in 10pt on 12pt Concorde Regular by
Falcon Oast Graphic Art Ltd.

Printed and bound in Spain by GraphyCems.

Note While all reasonable care has been taken
in the preparation of this publication, the pub-
lisher takes no responsibility for the use of the
methods or products described in the book.

Contents

1 ● Electronic navigation – do we need it? 1
Case history 1: *Kishmul of Ayr* • Case history 2: *Wahkuna*

2 ● New solutions, new problems 4
The shape of the Earth • Horizontal datums • An error? What error? • ...and different kinds of accuracy • Dilution of precision • Measuring error

3 ● Hardware, software and data 12
Man/machine interface • Controls • Menus and soft keys • Displays • Machine/machine interface • PC serial ports • NMEA 0183

4 ● What is GPS? 26
How it works • The satellites • Errors and accuracy • Improving the accuracy of GPS • Differential GPS • Other Satnavs

5 ● Using GPS 34
Initialising • Set-up options • Basic displays • Waypoint navigation • Route navigation • Routes and waypoints under way • Using waypoints to monitor position • Upwind sailing • GPS pilotage

6 ● Chart plotters 48
Raster charts • Vector charts • Passage planning on a plotter • Overlays

7 ● PCs on board 61
Laptops • Built-in PCs • Power supplies • Displays and controls • A look to the future

8 ● Echo sounders 65
How they work • Digital echo sounders • Forward-looking echo sounders • Installing an echo sounder • Calibrating an echo sounder

9 ● Logs 72
How it works • Installing a log • Calibrating a log

10 ● Electronic compasses 76
How a fluxgate • Installation • Self-correction

11 ● Radar – how it works 79
First principles • Main components • Display • Power consumption and safety

12 ● Radar – getting a picture 87
Switching on and setting up • Improving the picture • Stabilisation • Measuring tools

Contents

13 • Radar – what shows up?   **99**

Blind arcs and shadow sectors • What shows up? • Radar reflectors • Radar transponders • False echoes • Weather effects

14 • Using radar for collision avoidance   **109**

Radar and the Colregs • Assessing the risk • Closest point of approach • Finding course and speed • Advanced radar plotting • Guard zones • ARPA and MARPA

15 • Using radar for navigation and pilotage   **121**

Fix by radar bearings • Fix by radar ranges • Mixed fixes • Pilotage

Index   **131**

Electronic navigation – do we need it?

Human beings have been navigating the coastlines and oceans of the world for centuries. To hear some of the traditionalists talk, you'd think that nothing much had changed in that time – that the Vikings navigated by log, lead, and compass, and that ownership of a sextant connects you with an unbroken ancestry which began with the ancient Polynesians!

The truth is very different. The astro-navigation required of a 21st century Yachtmaster Ocean-qualified sailor has surprisingly little in common with the astro that guided escort ships to their convoys during the battle of the Atlantic. Even that was fundamentally different from the methods that were used in Victorian times, and just about the only thing it had in common with the celestial navigation of the centuries before Harrison invented his chronometer, was that both involved looking up at the sun and stars.

There's no doubt that the compass is the single most important navigation tool. Even now, the vast majority of yachts use a magnetic compass that Drake would probably recognise – though he, like any seaman before the 20th century, would probably be a bit puzzled by our use of degrees.

Less than 100 years before Drake, Columbus also used a compass in his search for the Indies. To him, though, it was new technology, and he treated it with suspicion. Like most navigators of his time,

he believed that it worked because some unseen force drew the needle towards the star of the Virgin Mary, so he was understandably worried when he found that his compass and the star didn't always seem to agree with each other. At first, he was inclined to believe the star, only gradually coming to realise that 'the star moves as the other stars...' and from that concluded that 'the needles always point truly'.

Of course, we now know that the needles don't 'always point truly' but the fact remains that after a slow start, the compass quickly became respectable.

Less than 30 years later, Magellan ventured deep into the Southern Ocean, where the familiar constellations were replaced by stars that no European had ever seen before. With little option other than to trust his compass, he took 35 spare compass needles with him – just as a modern ocean sailor might carry a bulk supply of batteries for his hand-held GPS!

Surprisingly, though, it was nearly 400 years before the problems of variation and deviation were properly understood and allowed for. By that time, Queen Victoria was already a widow, and the young Marconi was taking his first tottering steps. The first patents for radar and radio direction finding were less than a generation away, and another half century would see electronic navigation systems guiding airship bombers to their targets.

Electronic navigation isn't quite as new as we sometimes think it is – and maybe 'trad nav' isn't quite as traditional, either!

Case history 1: Kishmul of Ayr

Late in October 1999, the 28-foot *Kishmul of Ayr* was returning to Plymouth after a late season cruise to Guernsey and Cherbourg. The original plan had been to leave Cherbourg at midday on the Saturday, but the weather forecast on Friday evening persuaded her five-man crew to cut the trip short, leaving at midnight in the hope of getting home before the arrival of an approaching Atlantic depression.

It didn't quite work. By the time Plymouth breakwater light was spotted, the wind had already piped up to a force 7–8. It was rough, cold, and dark. Some of the crew were seasick, and they must all have been cold and tired – including the skipper, who had been at the helm for the previous four hours.

According to the report by the marine accident investigator, *'It isn't possible to know exactly what plan the skipper had in mind as he headed for the shelter of the Sound, but it involved keeping to seaward of a number of yellow firing range buoys lying off the Great Mew Stone.'* He probably intended to follow their line north-westward until it was safe to alter course to starboard towards the eastern entrance to Plymouth Sound. If so, he may have mistaken the middle buoy for the last one, because he seems to have altered course too soon. A few minutes later, just before 8 pm, *Kishmul* was being pounded against the unlit Renny Rocks, where she soon broke up.

Three of the crew were rescued by helicopter. Another managed to scramble ashore. The body of the skipper was recovered the following day.

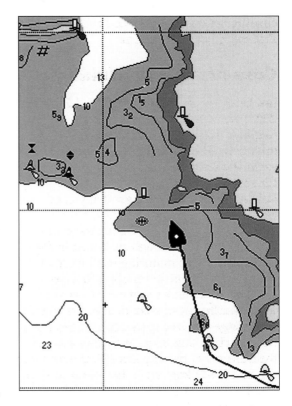

Fig 1 *Could an image like this, on the screen of a chart plotter, have saved the ill-fated Kishmul?*

A footnote to the accident report says that *Kishmul*'s GPS set was eventually recovered, and that it contained enough data to reconstruct the yacht's track over the final few minutes of the passage.

In other words, the GPS had been faithfully telling the skipper and crew that they were in the wrong place and heading in the wrong direction. Without plotting it on a chart, however, they couldn't have appreciated the significance of that information.

Just suppose that *Kishmul* had had a chart plotter in the cockpit. Confronted with a display like that in Fig 1, could the skipper have made the same mistake? Even without a plotter – a relatively pricey but primitive luxury in 1999 – there are simple tricks such as waypoint webs and GPS clearing bearings (explained in Chapter 5) that could have saved him.

Case history 2: Wahkuna

Just before nine, on the evening of 27 May 2003, the 900-foot container ship *P&O Nedlloyd Vespucci* left Antwerp on passage to Port Said. Eight hours later, the 47-foot yacht *Wahkuna* left Dielette, on the Cherbourg peninsula, heading for the Solent. Conditions were generally good, with a light wind and calm sea, but by 0900 the next morning the central part of the English Channel was shrouded in fog.

Wahkuna was motoring northward at about seven knots, in visibility that her crew estimated to be down to 50 metres, while *Nedlloyd Vespucci* headed westward. Her bridge watchkeepers couldn't see the bows of their own ship, but – like most of the other ships passing through the area at the time – she kept up to her usual service speed of 25 knots.

By about 1045, the two vessels were about six miles apart, and both could see each other on radar. According to *Vespucci*'s Automatic Radar Plotting Aid, *Wahkuna* was likely to cross nearly a mile ahead of her, but would then pass within a quarter of a mile of her starboard side.

Wahkuna's crew, however, saw a large contact whose range had reduced from six miles to three in little more than five minutes, and whose bearing didn't seem to be changing. Believing that they were on a collision course, *Wahkuna*'s skipper throttled back, intending to allow the other vessel to pass ahead.

A couple of minutes before eleven o'clock, *Wahkuna*'s *crew* heard a single fog signal, and saw the bows of a ship emerge from the fog.

The subsequent collision ripped away the mast and ten feet of *Wahkuna*'s bow. It was inevitable that she would soon sink, but by motoring hard astern her skipper was able to reduce the rate of flooding while he and his crew abandoned into their liferaft. The bridge team on *Vespucci*, meanwhile, were convinced that they had had a near miss. Still doing 25 knots, the ship carried on into the fog.

With characteristic even-handedness, the accident investigators of the Marine Accident Investigation Branch didn't single out either of the two vessels for blame: both were criticised for (amongst other things) making decisions based on scanty radar information and for not understanding the capabilities and limitations of their equipment.

New solutions, new problems

Fifty years ago, this chapter would have been unnecessary. Even twenty years ago, it would have seemed pretty pedantic. Back then, navigators – particularly yacht navigators – spent quite a bit of their time working out where they were, without much hope of achieving great accuracy. On a coastal passage, you'd be doing well if you knew your position to within a few hundred metres every once in a while, and on an offshore passage, errors could easily build up to several miles.

This lack of accuracy meant that we didn't need to bother too much about the precise definition of the words we use to describe where we are. Latitude and longitude were angles measured at the centre of the Earth, and for most practical purposes, that was good enough.

Accuracy and precision could safely be regarded as being almost synonymous – if you worked out your position accurately, you knew precisely where you were.

Neither of these things is true any longer. Simple assumptions such as 'the world is round' aren't good enough when we're dealing with navigation systems that offer worldwide coverage to an accuracy of a few metres.

The shape of the Earth

Forget what you learned at school! The Earth is *not* round! It isn't even an 'oblate spheroid', and it doesn't spin on its axis once every 24 hours.

It's an uneven and slightly flexible ball of

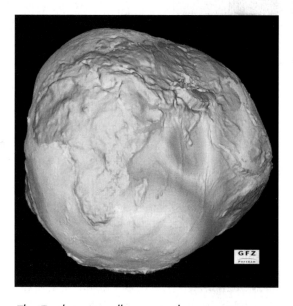

The Earth isn't really a smooth, geometric shape. This computer model of the Earth exaggerates the humps and hollows of the spheroid. The East coast of Africa is in the centre of the picture, and the UK is in the bulge, top left.

rock and water, wobbling its way through time and space. It's squashed at the poles, dented in the Indian Ocean, and bulges a bit in the western Pacific and north-east Atlantic, with countless other lumps and hollows in the form of mountains, valleys, and seas. Its axis of spin is constantly changing, and it has been gradually slowing down over the past few billion years.

Latitude and longitude

Finding a particular town or village in a road atlas of the whole country would be like looking for a needle in a haystack. To make the job easier, the publishers of the road atlas provide an index, which not only tells you which page to look on, but also indicates roughly where to look – usually by dividing the page up into a grid of squares. If Poole, for instance, is on page 8D3, that means it's on page eight, four squares along from the left (column D), and three squares up from the bottom (row 3).

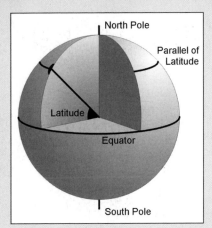
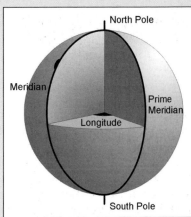

Fig 2 *Simple, traditional definitions of latitude and longitude refer to angles measured 'at the centre of the Earth'.*

Latitude and longitude serve much the same purpose, in that they provide a means of specifying position. The big difference – the thing that makes them so useful – is that they are universal: they relate to the whole world, and are based on standard reference points rather than to arbitrary lines drawn on the pages of a particular book.

The most obvious reference points to use for a worldwide reference system are the ends of the Earth's axis of spin: the North and South Poles. Exactly mid-way between them, running round the 'fattest' part of the Earth, is an imaginary line called the Equator, which provides the baseline for our measurement of latitude.

The formal definition of latitude is 'the angle which the perpendicular to the Earth's surface at a place makes with the plane of the Equator'. That, though, can be pretty difficult to understand, so a more common, simple definition is given as 'distance from the Equator, expressed as an angle measured at the centre of the Earth'.

If you were to draw a line through all the places that share the same latitude, you would end up with a line running round the world, parallel to the Equator, and called a parallel of latitude.

There's no correspondingly obvious baseline to use for measurements of longitude. We could draw any number of imaginary lines (called meridians) from pole to pole. They would all cross the Equator at right angles, but none of them would stand out as being particularly significant. For historical reasons, though, the one that passes through one particular telescope at the old Greenwich Observatory is called the Prime Meridian, and serves as the starting point for our measurements of longitude.

The definition of longitude is 'the angle between the plane of the prime meridian and the meridian passing through the place'.

The big snag with the concept of latitude and longitude is that it is based on the assumption that the poles and Equator are fixed, and that the Earth is a smooth, relatively simple geometrical shape.

Horizontal datums

The technology required to measure most of these imperfections, however, is relatively new, so over the years, mathematicians and mapmakers have come up with different ways of defining the shape of the Earth, while surveyors and navigators have found ways of fixing their position using whatever references were available to them – such as measuring the altitude of a star above the visible horizon.

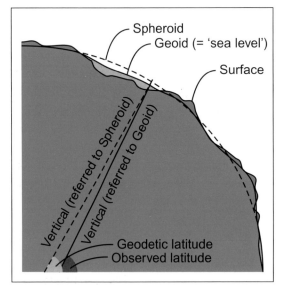

Fig 3 *Until recently, seamen and surveyors used the surface of the sea to define 'horizontal' and 'vertical'. So different parts of the Earth were surveyed using different 'centres' as the basis for latitude and longitude.*

Without realising it, they were basing their measurements of latitude and longitude on lots of different 'centres' of the Earth... which means that we now have lots of different graticules of latitude and longitude which don't quite marry up with each other. These are known as **horizontal datums**.

All current satellite navigation receivers use a relatively modern datum called WGS84 as their default. Most, however, are capable of converting to other datums, to suit the chart or map you may be using.

In European waters, you're also likely to come across:

- European Terrestrial Reference System (ETRS89), which is effectively identical to WGS84

- European Datum (ED50), used for older charts of Europe and the Channel Islands

- Ordnance Survey Great Britain (OSGB36), which is used for older charts of British waters.

▶▶ Differences between these datums vary from place to place, but are typically in the order of 100–200 metres.

All charts should give simple instructions for converting from WGS84 to the datum of the chart.

It is usually easier and more reliable to make sure that your GPS has been set up to convert positions to the datum of the chart you are using than to use the arithmetical conversion given on the chart.

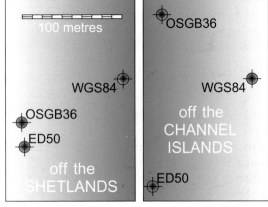

Fig 4 *Datum differences are not just academic! Using the wrong datum can introduce significant errors in position.*

Official (UKHO) charts are being converted to WGS84 or ETRS89, but it is a slow process. By the end of 2003, it had been completed for the southern half of mainland Britain, but charts of Scotland and parts of the North Sea are unlikely to be converted until 2008.

Worldwide, there are over 300 charts in the Admiralty 'standard' series for which the datum is still unknown.

GPS altitude

Almost all GPS receivers are capable of displaying altitude; it's a by-product of the way they calculate their position.

Unfortunately, GPS altitude is of no practical value for the marine navigator, because it's inherently less accurate than GPS position, and is therefore insufficiently accurate to take the place of tidal calculations, and because it does not relate to height above or below sea level or chart datum, but to a mathematical 'model' of the shape of the Earth (called the spheroid).

Sea level (the geoid) is over 100m below the spheroid in places, and up to 85m above it in others. In the UK, it is between 45 metres and 60 metres above the spheroid. The actual surface, of course, varies from several thousand metres below the geoid to several thousand metres above it.

An error? What error?

If you sit still with a hand-held GPS set, and make a note of the position it shows every minute for a couple of hours, you'll almost certainly end up with a pattern something like that in Fig 5. The overall effect is rather as though someone has fired a shotgun at a target: most of the fixes are clustered close together, but others are more spread out, and one or two stragglers are quite some distance from the main group.

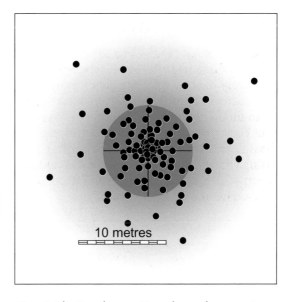

Fig 5 *Plotting the position shown by a stationary GPS receiver produces a pattern like this.*

The reason is that GPS – like every navigation system before or since – is subject to a variety of errors. GPS works by measuring the time taken for a radio signal to travel from each of several satellites to the receiver. There's a much more detailed description in Chapter 4, but even from that condensed version, it's easy to see how errors creep in. For example:

- the satellites may not be exactly where they say they are;

- their signals may not have reached us by the shortest possible route;

- the measurement of distance may be wrong; or

- we may have mis-read the display.

These are just four examples from a considerably longer list, but all are quite independent of each other. This means that sometimes they will add together, to produce a large total error, but will sometimes cancel each other out.

Academic navigators classify errors into three groups: faults, systematic errors, and random errors.

Faults

Faults include things such as equipment failure and operator error. It's easier to say 'they shouldn't happen', than to make sure they don't. Their saving grace is that in most cases they are easy to spot because they are large, short-lived, or obvious.

It's pretty clear, for instance, that if a GPS set's display goes blank, there's a fault! It's very nearly as obvious that if you plot your position and find that you seem to be exactly 60 miles north of where you expected to be, then you've probably mis-read the latitude display.

Systematic errors

Systematic (or 'systemic') errors follow some regular pattern. This means that they can be predicted and allowed for. The classic examples are variation and devia-tion of a magnetic compass. The simplest systematic errors are constant, so they are often described as 'fixed errors'. A simple example is an echo sounder that has not been calibrated to allow for the distance between the transducer and the surface of the water – and which can always be expected to show slightly less than the true depth.

Random errors

Random errors, on the other hand, change quickly and unpredictably. While the boffins generally do their best to reduce or eliminate them by means such as differential GPS (see page 31), navigators have to learn to live with them. In practice, this means we have to acknowl-edge their existence, and allow a suitable safety margin between us and any nearby hazards.

...and different kinds of accuracy

Different kinds of error lead to different kinds of accuracy.

Absolute accuracy

Absolute (or predictable) accuracy refers to how accurately a position can be indicated, usually in terms of latitude and longitude. It's the kind of accuracy you need in order to find a harbour entrance in fog. It's prob-ably what most of us are thinking of when we talk about 'accuracy', but it's only in the last twenty years or so that we've come close to achieving it.

Relative accuracy

If you could measure the distance from your mooring to the pub with a long tape measure, how would that compare with the distance between the two as indicated by your navigation system?

That's what we mean by relative accu-racy – the accuracy with which one position can be compared with another.

It wouldn't matter, in this case, if your navigator shows that your mooring is two miles east of where you really are, so long as it is consistent about it, and puts the pub two miles further east as well.

Good relative accuracy can be achieved by a system with large systemic errors, so long as its random errors are small.

Repeatability

Repeatability – or repeatable accuracy – is a system's ability to guide you back to the same spot, time after time. It's particularly important for people like fishermen and divers, who don't really need to know exactly where they left their crab pots or newly-discovered wreck, but certainly want to be able to get back to exactly the same spot.

Good repeatable accuracy can be achieved by a system with large systemic errors, even if they vary quite a lot from place to place, so long as they don't change from time to time.

Precision

Precision has very little to do with accuracy. If anything, in real life as in politics, the opposite is usually true, and the most precise, apparently authoritative statement is the one that turns out to be least reliable!

A good definition of precision is the level of refinement to which a value is stated. In practice that usually means 'how many numbers after the decimal point?' Most GPS sets, for instance, give positions to three places of decimals. In the UK, that's a precision of 1.8m in latitude and 1.2m in longitude. Errors inherent in the system, however, mean that the vast majority of standard, stand-alone GPS fixes will be considerably less accurate than this. It makes sense, in other words, to ignore the last place of decimals, because it gives a misleading impression of accuracy.

Dilution of precision

Dilution of precision, however, has a very direct effect on accuracy.

When two or three measurements are combined to produce a fix, their errors are exaggerated. This applies to all position fixing methods that involve more than one measurement, but it's probably easiest to visualise in the case of a fix taken by plotting radar ranges (see Chapter 15, page 124).

The basic assumption is that if the radar shows a headland two miles away, then our position must lie somewhere on a circle whose centre is at the headland and whose radius is two miles. The snag is that although radar is pretty good at measuring ranges, it isn't perfect. If we believe our measurement to be accurate to 30m, each of those circular position lines should be drawn with a thick pencil, to represent a

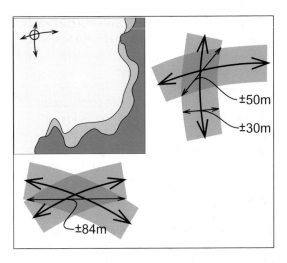

Fig 6 *A radar fix whose position lines cut at a shallow angle produces a much larger area of uncertainty than one whose position lines cut at a large angle. This effect is called dilution of precision.*

line 60m wide – a margin for error of 30m on each side of the idealised thin line.

When you do the same with a second headland, to get a second position line, and allow a similar margin for error, the end result is a dark-shaded diamond shape in which these two broad position lines intersect. The diamond, however, is considerably bigger than the range errors which caused it. It gets bigger still if the position lines intersect at very shallow angles.

This effect is called 'dilution of precision' or DOP. DOP=2 means that the error of the fix may be twice the error in the original measurement. DOP=10 means the accuracy of the fix is ten times worse than accuracy of the range measurement.

For three-dimensional systems – including GPS – it is quite common to find several different kinds of DOP:
PDOP = *Position Dilution of Precision* – concerned with all three dimensions
HDOP = *Horizontal Dilution of Precision* – concerned only with horizontal position

VDOP = *Vertical Dilution of Precision* – concerned only with height

TDOP = *Time Dilution of Precision* – concerned only with time

GDOP = *Geometric Dilution of Precision* – similar to PDOP, but includes errors in the fourth dimension (time)

Measuring error

If you know where you are, and where your GPS says you are, it's quite easy to measure its error. The trouble is that in real life, we don't know where we are, because we're relying on the GPS to tell us.

It would be very helpful, though, if we had some idea how wrong the GPS position was likely to be. If nothing else, we'd know how wide a margin we should allow for error.

Faced with a pattern like that in Fig 5, it's difficult to quote a single figure for accuracy. It might be tempting to suggest that it's accurate to a metre or so, on the basis that there are several fixes that are almost spot on. To do that, though, would be like suggesting that all human beings can run a four minute mile when the truth is that some can, but there are very many more who can't.

Alternatively, we might say that it's accurate to about 20m or so – on the basis that there are no fixes more than 20m from the true position. But what would happen if we stayed longer? There might be other fixes that are worse still!

The solution is to draw a sequence of expanding circles around the true position, until we find one that encloses 50% of all the fixes – like the darkest circle in the diagram. This is sometimes called the CEP50%, or 'Circle of Error Probability 50%', because if you drew a circle that size around any single fix, there's a 50% probability of your true position lying within the circle.

For most civilian GPS receivers, the CEP50% is about 7m. This is a useful indication of the sort of accuracy we could expect, but it's not a very good indication of the margin for error we should allow. For that, we need to choose a bigger circle, because by using a bigger circle we can have more confidence that we are somewhere within it.

One possibility is the '1σ' circle. Sigma 'σ' is statisticians' shorthand for 'standard deviation' or the 'root mean square error' (dRMS). One virtue of the 1σ circle is that its size can be calculated relatively easily, without having to plot thousands of fixes or draw circles[1]. For statisticians, it is also useful as a basis for more sophisticated calculations, while for navigators it is a good indication of the practical value of a navigation system because it tends to 'reward' a consistent performer with a lower figure than an erratic one.

The snag is that the 1σ circle is not much bigger than CEP50%, and includes only about 67% of all fixes. It would be nice to have rather more than 67% confidence in the accuracy of your navigation system!

A particularly useful and widespread measure of accuracy is the 2σ (or 2dRMS) circle, which is twice the diameter of the 1σ circle. For a system like GPS, whose errors are mostly random, it encloses about 95% of all fixes. This not only suits the boffins, but also gives ordinary navigators a good idea of how bad a bad GPS fix is likely to be. Bear in mind, though, that it's not the only measure of accuracy.

The now-obsolete Decca system, for instance, was usually quoted at the 1σ level, whereas the accuracy of the Russian Glonass satellite system is quoted at the 3σ level – equivalent to a 99.7% level of confidence.

---

[1] Measure all the errors, square them, take the mean of the squared errors, and find the square root of the mean.

and finally...

Remember that many of the charts we use nowadays, whether printed on paper or stored in the electronic memory of a chart plotting system, are based on surveys carried out before such accurate position fixing systems as GPS were available. In parts of the Pacific, the most up to date charts available now were originally published at the end of the 19th century, and there are many more charts which are based on old surveys or for which the horizontal datum is unknown.

3

Hardware, software and data

All computer systems – including the vast majority of electronic navigation equipment – are made up of three main types of component: *hardware*, *software*, and *data*.

Hardware is usually the most obvious: it is the solid, physical machine that you carry out of the shop when you buy a computer or a GPS receiver. The 'computer' bit of it is the **central processing unit.** This is a silicon 'chip' – often about the size of a postage stamp – that includes thousands of microscopic electronic switches which between them are able to manage and process the information supplied to the chip in the form of tiny electrical pulses.

You could think of it as being like the assembly line at the heart of a factory. Like the assembly line, however, the CPU isn't much good on its own however, so in a typical PC, it is usually mounted on a complicated-looking printed circuit board called a **motherboard**, surrounded by other components. These usually include one or more kinds of **memory** to store the raw

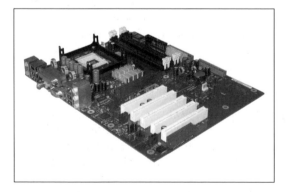

The motherboard at the heart of a typical PC.

materials and the finished products, a power supply and fan to keep the CPU running and to stop it overheating, and various smaller processors to run the computer's own domestic systems – making sure the fan switches on and off at the right time, that its battery is properly charged, and so on.

Finally, there are the **ports** which – like the loading bays of a factory – are the computer's links to the outside world. They take information in, from the keyboard and mouse, or from other equipment such as a GPS receiver, and send the processed information out to a screen or printer.

Software is far less conspicuous than hardware. In many cases, it has no physical form at all, and you may not even be aware of having bought it. In others, you may have spent several hundred pounds on a cardboard box which turns out to contain nothing more than a compact disc and some paperwork.

What you have bought is a set of very detailed instructions – which would certainly be gibberish to you, even if you could see them, but which should make complete sense to the computer – which tell it exactly how to handle the data it is given.

You may occasionally come across the term '**firmware**'. In principle, firmware does much the same job as software, because it determines how the computer manipulates data. The big difference is that firmware is permanently built into the hardware. A good example is in a computer keyboard, in which the firmware identifies which key has been pressed, and translates that into a string of electrical pulses that the computer can understand.

Data is perhaps the most important and valuable of the three components, because although it's the one that we most often take for granted, it is the very reason that the other two exist!

It takes many different forms, including the human input from a keyboard or control panel, automated input from a GPS set or radar scanner unit, or stored information (often called a database) from a CD (compact disc) or a memory cartridge. Output data is most often used to drive a display unit, which turns it into a form that human beings can understand, but other types of output data can be used to control other machines, such as steering systems or engines, or communications equipment.

Man/machine interface

Almost all machines need some means of communicating with their human operators. The geeks might call it a man-machine interface, comparable with the machine-machine interface that allows a satellite navigator (for instance) to communicate with an autopilot. In more everyday language, though, we tend to talk about controls and displays. The distinction between a control system and a display, however, is becoming blurred: many control systems involve selection from a 'menu' of choices shown on the display, and some even involve touching the screen, rather than pressing buttons or twiddling knobs.

Controls

Buttons v knobs
Buttons or keys (which you press) and knobs (which you twist) have completely different strengths and weaknesses. In general terms, knobs are best at progressive functions, such as changing the volume of a loudspeaker or the brightness of a display.

Keys or buttons are better at non-progressive functions, such as switching something on or off, or picking one from a number of clearly separated choices – such as picking out the letters required to type a name.

In marine equipment, waterproofing can be an issue. Knobs can certainly be made waterproof, but it's much more difficult and expensive to achieve a good seal around the shaft of a knob than it is to put a flexible waterproof membrane between a keypad and the microswitches that it operates. Consequently we've seen a general trend towards keys and buttons, and away from knobs.

OBOJ systems
There can't be much doubt that the simplest control system of all is a labelled button which does a single job, such as turning on a light, selecting low power on a radio, or deleting the heading mark on a radar (see page 93).

The snag with one-button-one-job control systems is that for anything but the simplest of devices, the sheer number of buttons involved takes up a lot of space. Labelling them also becomes a problem for the manufacturer, while finding the right one amongst so many can be difficult for the user.

Multifunction buttons
One step on from one-button-one-job control panels are those in which each button can perform several different functions, depending on whether it's pressed and released, pressed and held, pressed twice, or pressed at the same time as some other key.

Generally speaking, these systems work well where there is some consistent relationship between the various functions performed by each key. On a typewriter or computer keyboard, for instance, it makes complete sense for the <shift> <q> to produce a capital Q, because the <shift> key

A well-designed 'user interface' makes operation easy, by using a sensible mixture of clearly-labelled buttons and knobs.

has exactly the same effect on all the letter keys.

It is rather harder to justify dual function or multifunction function keys where there is no obvious relationship between the various functions performed by each key. It may be just about acceptable, so long as there aren't too many keys, and each one is clearly labelled with *all* its various functions.

Watch out, though, for the kind of equipment that boasts a long list of features and functions but has no visible means of controlling them all!

Pointing tools

Display technology has developed in leaps and bounds over the past few years, so now, even a £100 fish-finder is likely to have a display that is quite capable of showing easily-legible text. This has opened the door to menu systems, in which you control the machine by selecting the function you want from a list displayed on the screen.

To do this, however, you need some way of telling the machine which item you want. One day, perhaps, we shall be using voice-activated systems, which really do let you 'talk' to the machine. At the moment, though, the usual system involves some kind of pointing device.

At its simplest, this is no more than a pair of keys, marked with **up and down arrows**. By pressing one or the other of the two keys, you move up or down a list displayed on the screen. In most cases, you then have to press another button to confirm your selection.

Up-and-down selectors work well for relatively simple lists, such as the choice of channels on a radio, or for the list of horizontal datums available on a GPS receiver.

Much more sophisticated choices can be made, though, if you can point to any part of the screen you like. This involves using four (or sometimes eight) **cursor control keys** to move a marker on the screen in any direction. Not only does this allow you to choose from far more varied menus; it also allows you to highlight part of the screen image on a chart plotter, for instance, in order to ask it for more information about a particular buoy. Some equipment designers cover the four or eight microswitches with one large button instead of several separate ones, but it's largely a cosmetic difference; the principle is exactly the same.

There can't be many people who aren't familiar with the computer **mouse**. A creature of the Sixties, the mouse, in its simplest form, consists of a hollow body containing a small rubber ball and a couple of rollers or wheels. As you move the mouse over any firm surface, the ball rolls, and as it does so turns one or both of the rollers. Moving a roller has exactly the same effect as holding down one of a group of four-way arrow keys – it moves the cursor or highlight on the display. Most mice have a number of buttons, at least one of which serves to confirm your selection from a menu.

A **tracker ball** can be visualised as an upside down mouse, in which you roll the ball with your fingers instead of by moving the whole mouse. A **joystick** does much the same, except that it consists of a more-or-less vertical lever that can be moved in any direction.

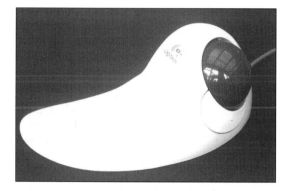

Anyone who uses a PC is likely to be familiar with a mouse – but a tracker ball is a much better pointing tool at sea.

Although cheap and simple mice are still available, there are considerably more sophisticated versions around, some of which have no moving parts. Even so, they are best suited to office use or to large vessels with plenty of space. For marine use, tracker balls or joysticks are generally better, because they take up less space and are less likely to fall off the chart table when the boat moves.

Track pads are popular on laptop computers, and look like little flat rubber mats. Underneath, however, is any of several different types of sensor. When you put your finger on the track pad and move it, it has much the same effect as moving a mouse. Some people love track pads, but they do take a little getting used to, and some types

don't work if you have wet hands or are wearing gloves.

Touch screens are like transparent track pads, built into (or fitted over) the display screen. They work rather differently than track pads, though, because they respond to touch rather than to movement. This makes them particularly suitable for choosing from menus, so are becoming very popular for things like cashpoints, supermarket checkouts, and airport information centres. Like trackpads, though, they can't all cope with wet hands or gloves, and they may not be accurate enough for some navigational purposes.

Do you speak mouse?

Mice, and their close relations, the trackball, trackpad, and joystick are so fundamental to almost any computer system that everyone should be aware of a few basic words of mouse jargon.

Cursor: a mark – often in the shape of an arrow or a cross – that can be moved around the computer screen by means of the mouse.

Highlight: a word or symbol distinguished from those around it by being displayed in a different colour or against a different-coloured background.

Point: move the mouse so as to position the cursor at a particular spot or to highlight a particular word or symbol.

Click: press the main or only button on the mouse (usually the one on the left).

Right click: press the secondary button on the mouse (usually the one on the right).

Drag: move the mouse while holding the left mouse button down. Depending what you are doing at the time, this can be used to highlight an area on the screen (such as when 'zooming in' on a chart plotter) or to move an object on the screen (such as a waypoint) or to highlight a group of items on a list (such as a group of waypoints that you want to copy or delete).

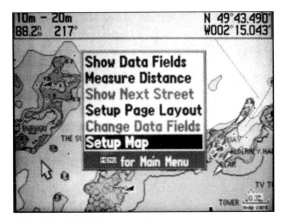

Menus offer a range of control choices. You usually have to highlight one by using the tracker ball or cursor control keys, before confirming it by pressing another key.

Menus and soft keys

Menus are something that people love to hate – and with good reason: trying to control a piece of electronic equipment with a badly-designed menu system can be desperately frustrating. On the other hand, it's fair to say that without menus, we would be stuck with pretty primitive equipment. Hand-held devices, in particular, would be very restricted.

The principle of a menu is simple: it presents you with a list of choices, from which you take your pick. This usually involves pressing a button labelled <menu> to reveal the menu, using arrow keys or some other kind of pointing device to highlight the function you want, and then pressing an <enter> key or the left mouse button to confirm your selection. Sometimes, that's all there is to it.

Often, however, your initial selection leads into another menu, which may lead into another – and so on. This is where frustration can creep in, because although you probably know what you are trying to achieve, it may not be obvious how to get to it. A well-designed menu will help you, but it still takes time.

An increasingly popular variation on the menu idea uses what are known as **soft keys**. Soft keys are push-buttons without labels. There are usually four or five of them, arranged alongside or underneath the display, with the menu choices appearing

The five 'soft keys' below the display of this radar have labels that appear on the screen itself. In effect, the soft keys are just another way of selecting items from a menu.

on the screen alongside or above them. Each time you make a selection, by pressing the appropriate soft key, the labels change, to present you with the next sequence of choices.

Displays

Most electronic navigation equipment exists in order to supply us with information, so it would be pretty useless if it didn't have some means of giving us that information in a form that we can understand. With very few exceptions (such as the audio compasses, used by blind sailors, and some communications systems which print out 'hard' copies on paper) that means they need a display of some sort.

Like control systems, displays vary enormously, but they can be divided into three main groups:

- Analogue
- Digital
- Graphic

Analogue v digital v graphic

Analogue displays are sometimes regarded as 'simple' or 'old-fashioned', because they use the movement of a pointer or marker against a scale to indicate a measurement such as depth or speed. They certainly don't look very precise; the pointer seldom points straight at any of the markings on the dial, and often seems to flicker. This, however, may be an accurate indication of the true situation: the true depth for instance is seldom an exact number of metres, and usually changes as the boat moves over lumps and bumps in the sea bed. Analogue displays are so good at conveying approximate or fluctuating information at a glance that some electronic instruments now have 'quasi analogue' displays in which digital information is displayed on a graphic replica of an analogue display.

An analogue display is good at conveying approximate or fluctuating information such as this wind direction indicator.

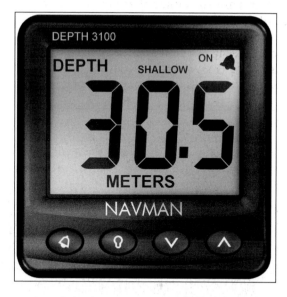

A digital display gives a clear and unambiguous read-out.

Digital displays have the virtue of precision, and of giving a clear and unambiguous measurement. The classic example is the latitude and longitude read-out of a GPS set: 50° 47.17N may be a lot more useful than the 'about three quarters of the way between 50° 40' and 50° 50'' that might be given by an analogue display. They are also generally cheaper to make and inherently more reliable.

Graphic displays, capable of representing information in the form of a picture, are fast becoming the norm for almost all electronic equipment from a £100 fish-finder upwards. As their popularity grows, their prices fall, so they become even more popular. In most cases the display is made up of a pattern of square or rectangular blobs, called pixels, each of which can be individually lightened or darkened. In some cases, there may be only a few hundred pixels, but even this is enough to produce simple pictures or a few lines of text or numbers. At the other extreme some computer monitors use over three million pixels to produce screen images that are almost as clear as photographs.

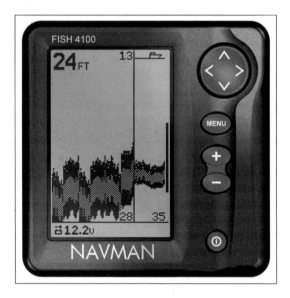

A graphic display gives information in pictorial form, like this fish-finder showing a graph of the changing depth of water.

Light emitting diodes (LEDs)

A diode is one of the simplest types of electronic valve, designed primarily to allow electricity to flow in one direction, but not the other. Originally, they looked rather like light bulbs, with various filaments and metal grids enclosed in a glass tube. Nowadays, however, virtually all diodes are 'solid state', made of an insulating material called aluminium-gallium-arsenide, with carefully chosen impurities such as silicon, which give it its special ability to conduct electricity in one direction only.

Any flow of electricity involves moving electrons from one atom to another. In a diode, however, this process of rearranging electrons and atoms produces light. In the ordinary diodes inside a radio, for instance, the light produced is way outside the relatively narrow band of colour that we can see – it's usually in the 'infra red' spectrum – and most of it is absorbed by the material of the diode itself. LEDs, however, use chemicals chosen for their ability to produce visible light, and are mounted inside a tiny transparent case.

The end result is something like a tiny light bulb – except that it is very much more efficient than any conventional light bulb, because it doesn't waste energy producing heat. It also lasts very much longer, because there is nothing inside that can melt or break. Single LEDs are often used as indicator lights, to show whether something is switched on, for instance, but groups of LEDs can also be used to form the shapes of letters or numbers. In the Seventies and Eighties, they were widely used in Decca Navigator position fixers, for instance, and were still serving the same purpose in some of the first GPS sets.

Nowadays, though, their role in navigation equipment is once more confined almost entirely to indicator lights.

Cathode ray tubes (CRTs)

There can't be many homes that don't have

at least one cathode ray tube – probably in a corner of the sitting room, inside the TV set.

Essentially, it consists of a glass 'tube' shaped like a funnel, or a ship's decanter. At the end of the neck of the decanter is a device known as an 'electron gun', because its purpose is to fire electrons along the tube. The inside of the 'bottom' of the decanter – the TV 'screen' – is treated with a phosphorescent coating, which glows when it is struck by an electron.

As it stands, this set up would leave most of the screen dark, with just a single bright spot in the middle where the beam of electrons hit it. In order to make a picture, the electron beam has to move, and has to vary in intensity.

A **radial scan CRT** is used in some old-fashioned radars. It uses a set of electromagnets to bend the beam of electrons, moving the bright spot out towards the edge of the screen, then allowing it to ping back to the centre. The whole process happens very quickly; in a radar set at a typical operating range of 6 miles, for instance, the whole process takes less than a tenth of a millisecond!

At the same time, the magnets are rotating around the neck of the tube, so the next time it happens, about a thousandth of a second later, the beam is bent in a slightly different direction. This, however, is a relatively slow process, with the magnets taking two or three seconds to achieve a complete rotation. The end result is that the picture is built up as a series of lines, radiating outwards from the centre of the screen like the spokes of a wheel.

This is useful in a radar because that is exactly how a radar set receives its information from the rotating scanner, but it has a couple of major drawbacks. They both arise from the fact that it takes several seconds to build up a complete picture. One obvious snag is that it takes several seconds for the picture to change. The other is that

in order to display a complete picture, the phosphor coating of the screen has to carry on glowing for several seconds after it has been struck by the electron beam. This is perfectly possible, but only if you are prepared to put up with a very dim picture. That is why old-fashioned radars had to be fitted with light-tight hoods, so the operator could see the faint image without being dazzled by background light.

Daylight viewing radars, CRT chart plotters, computers, and televisions all use a different technique, known as raster scan. A **raster CRT** works on exactly the same principles, but instead of a single rotating magnet, uses two pairs of magnets, one of which deflects the beam from side to side, while the other moves it up and down. In the case of a television, the beam flicks from one side to the other, changing in intensity as it goes, to build up the first of several hundred 'lines' that make up the complete picture. Then it snaps back to where it started from, but slightly lower down the screen, to repeat the process with the second line.

In a raster CRT, the whole thing happens very quickly; a UK-standard TV set, for instance, paints 625 lines in a twenty-fifth of a second. Not only does this allow the picture to be updated 25 times a second; it also means that the phosphor coating inside the tube never has to glow for more than 0.04 second. This, in turn, means that it can be made to glow brightly enough to be seen in daylight.

Even so, and despite their relatively low cost that stems from their enormous popularity in TV sets and computers, raster scan CRTs are disappearing from marine electronics, because they are inefficient and relatively fragile compared with liquid crystal displays (LCDs).

Liquid crystal displays (LCDs)

In everyday existence, we come across matter in only three forms: solid, liquid, or gas.

Liquid crystals, however, are artificially-produced 'designer molecules', with some of the characteristics of liquids but with a regular crystal structure like that of a solid.

Left to its own devices, the long, straight molecules of a liquid crystal lie parallel with each other, like the sleepers in a railway line. This is called the 'nematic' state.

A liquid crystal display (LCD) consists of a thin layer of liquid crystal, sandwiched between several other layers designed to harness its peculiar talents.

The two layers immediately outside the liquid crystal are etched with very fine grooves, which attract the molecules at the end of each strand of liquid crystal. The grooves in these 'alignment layers', however, are not parallel to each other. The result is that each ribbon-like strand of liquid crystal is given a definite twist.

All three layers are then sandwiched between polarising filters. Like the alignment layers, the polarising filters are arranged at 90° to each other, so you'd expect the whole sandwich to be opaque, as one filter cuts out all except horizontally-polarised light while the other cuts out all except vertically-polarised. The clever bit is that the twisted rows of liquid crystal molecules twist the polarisation of the light as it passes through them on its way from one filter to the other – making the sandwich transparent.

It's still possible to make some parts of the sandwich opaque again, by applying a small electric current through the liquid crystal. Wherever the electricity flows, the nematic arrangement is disrupted and the crystal loses its ability to twist the polarisation of light.

There are basically two ways of controlling which bits of the display receive an electric current, and which don't. Until a few years ago, all LCDs had a grid of vertical wires on one side of the sandwich and a grid of horizontal wires on the other. It's called a 'passive matrix'. A voltage was applied to one of the horizontal wires, and the vertical wires switched 'on' or 'off' to decide where the electricity was allowed to flow through the display to produce a dark cell. Then the process was repeated for each horizontal wire in turn.

Better, more modern displays use what are known as **thin film transistors (TFTs)** as miniature switches to control each pixel individually. It means that the whole display can react almost instantaneously, instead of line by line – but it's expensive: a 7-in monochrome display might well be 640 pixels high and 480 pixels wide: over 300,000 pixels, each controlled by its own transistor. For a colour display, each pixel needs three transistors, so the total increases to almost a million.

The final ingredient in the sandwich is the light itself.

Reflective displays use external light, which passes through the display to a reflective backing, and is then reflected back out again. They work well in sunlight, because the display naturally gets brighter as the natural light increases. They're not too clever at night, though!

Transmissive displays use internal light. Of course they use a bit more power than reflective displays, but are much better at night. The trouble is that their relatively dim internal lighting can't compete with bright daylight.

Transflective displays are a compromise, with internal lighting and a reflective backing. Like all compromises, they aren't quite as good as the more specialised products in extreme conditions, but they are far better all-rounders, and are much the best choice for marine instruments. Unfortunately, they seldom look quite as good as transmissive displays when you see them at boat shows or in dimly-lit showrooms!

Display sizes

Display sizes are usually quoted in inches, measured across the diagonal. This isn't deliberately misleading, but it produces some strange effects:

14=15?

An LCD diagonal represents the visible size of the screen, whereas a CRT ('TV-style') display size is based on the nominal diameter of the cathode ray tube. A 14-in LCD produces the same size picture as a 15-in CRT.

4x7=14?

A 14-in LCD is about as big as an A4 sheet of paper. Fold the A4 sheet in half, and it's about the size of a 10-in screen. Fold in half again, and it's about the size of a 7-in screen.

Machine/machine interface

In the early days of small-craft electronics, each instrument was completely separate: the log, echo sounder, and position fixer (this was in the days before GPS) got on with their own jobs, without being connected to any of the others other than by sharing a power supply. By the Seventies, however, it was becoming pretty obvious that it would be a good idea if position fixers could communicate directly with autopilots.

Some manufacturers set up their own systems for doing this, but the real breakthrough came in 1980, when the National Marine Electronics Association (of America) introduced their NMEA 0180 standard. For the first time, customers could reasonably expect a position fixer produced by one company to be able to communicate directly with an autopilot produced by another.

The NMEA 0180 standard was improved in 1982, to produce NMEA 0182, but it was already becoming clear that the principle of intercommunication or 'interfacing'

could usefully be extended to much more than position fixers and autopilots.

The NMEA 0183 standard, introduced in 1983, involved a radical re-think of the system, but made it possible for almost any piece of marine equipment to communicate with any other, or with a PC.

NMEA 0183 has been updated and improved over the years, but it has served us astonishingly well. Nevertheless, by the tail end of the 20th century, it was starting to look a bit creaky, so NMEA set to work on a new standard for the new millennium, to be called NMEA 2000.

At present, however (2005), it looks as though NMEA 2000 may have been too late in coming: the number of manufacturers has reduced since the Eighties, as many have combined or been taken over, and most of them have reverted to using their own proprietary communication systems between their own instruments. NMEA 0183, however, is still going strong.

PC serial ports

If you look at the back of any personal computer, you'll see lots of different sockets to take an assortment of plugs to connect the computer to peripheral equipment such as a keyboard, mouse, loudspeakers, display, and so on. There are usually, nowadays, at least three others, of which the smallest and most sophisticated is a USB port.

Its very sophistication means that the USB port need not concern us; if you have a piece of equipment with a USB plug on the end, you can plug it into a computer's USB port and there's a very good chance that it will work. The chances are even better if you've read the instruction manual first.

The other two are much bigger, and are called the serial and parallel ports.

To appreciate the difference between them, you first need to know that computers communicate with each other in a code made up of pulses of low-voltage electricity. In some ways, it's rather like Morse code and the early electric telegraph, except that it all happens very much faster.

A PC's serial port is a simple but rather slow way of exchanging data with other PCs or navigation equipment.

The 'Morse' code, in this case, is called ASCII (American Standard Code for Information Interchange), in which every letter, number, character and punctuation mark is represented by a sequence of eight electrical pulses. A connection in which the pulses follow one another 'in series' is called a **serial** port. Now, although computers can send and receive pulses of electricity very quickly, the process of sending and receiving a large amount of information through a serial port can take a measurable amount of time.

One way to speed it up is by sending all eight pulses simultaneously. That is how a **parallel** port works, and partly explains why it has so many pins.

Back in the early Eighties, however, marine equipment interfaces didn't really need speed; they needed simplicity. So although NMEA 0183 is not identical to the RS 232 and RS 422 that govern computer serial ports, it is very similar, and in many cases it is easy to connect marine equipment that uses NMEA 0183 to the serial port of a PC.

Interface voltages

One important difference between the NMEA 0183 interface used by marine instruments and the RS 232 interface used by computers is in the voltages they use.

In NMEA 0183, a voltage of between +4v and +15v represents a 'zero' pulse, and a voltage of between +0.5 and −15 is a 'unit' pulse.

In RS 232, a 'zero' pulse is represented by a voltage between +5v and +15v, while a 'unit' is represented by a voltage of between −5v and −15v.

So an NMEA listener should always understand an RS 232 talker, because the transmitted pulses always fall within the tolerances accepted by the NMEA standard. Problems can arise, however, if an NMEA talker uses anything between +0.5v and −5v to signify a 'unit'. In most cases, the PC will interpret anything that is 'not a zero' as being a unit − but it can't be guaranteed.

The solution is to use an NMEA/RS 232 converter cable, available from specialist marine electronics suppliers.

NMEA 0183

Like the ASCII code that computers use to talk to each other, the NMEA 0183 code consists of a series of electrical pulses, usually at between 0–5v. The pulses are delivered in groups of eight, with each group representing particular letters, figures, and punctuation marks. For instance:

▶▶ 00100100 represents a dollar sign, while 01000111 represents the letter G, and 00110101 represents the figure 5.

Like the letters and punctuation marks that make up normal writing, the various characters of the NMEA code are assembled into words and sentences, but with far

```
                    NMEA  DATA
$GPGLL,5055.1659,N,00118.2341,W,182119.00,A*16

33,M,+049,M,00,0000*7D
$GPVTG,175.3,T,,,000.1,N,000.2,K*2E
$GPRMC,182118,A,5055.1660,N,00118.2342,W,000.1,175
.,090704,,*3F
$GPGLL,5055.1660,N,00118.2342,W,182118.00,A*1E
$GPGSV,3,1,10,09,73,289,46,26,41,150,00,07,35,084,
45,18,34,257,00*71
$GPGSV,3,2,10,05,32,219,00,29,30,148,00,22,29,298,
00,28,17,050,42*75
$GPGSV,3,3,10,31,15,039,36,14,02,314,00,00,00,000,
00,00,00,000,00*70
$GPGGA,182119,5055.1659,N,00118.2341,W,1,04,02,+00
33,M,+049,M,00,0000*75
$GPVTG,175.8,T,,,000.1,N,000.2,K*25
$GPRMC,182119,A,5055.1659,N,00118.2341,W,000.1,175
.,090704,,*37


ENTER TO START
ZOOM IN TO CHANGE PORT          Port: NMEA1
```

NMEA data, seen here in the form in which it is received.

stricter rules of punctuation and grammar. Every sentence, for instance, must begin with a dollar sign and end with a line feed (an instruction to start a new line), and each word must be separated from the one after it by a comma. The first word must always consist of five letters, of which the first two identify the type of equipment that has sent the message, while the remaining three identify the content and structure of that particular sentence. A very common NMEA sentence, for instance, might read:

▸▸ $GPGLL,5047.17,N,00118.57,W,143726,A<LF>

It means that the data has come from a GPS (GP), and that it is the current

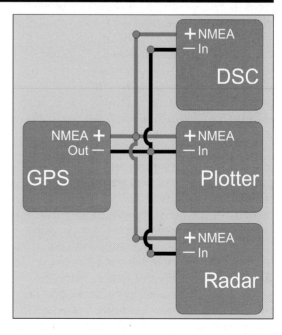

Fig 7 *Several 'listeners' can be connected to one 'talker', but not vice versa.*

latitude and longitude (GLL). The next few figures and numbers represent the latitude, longitude, and time, followed by the letter A to indicate that there is nothing wrong with the information – that the GPS is receiving the signals from enough satellites, and so on.

The physical connection between the equipment transmitting the information (called the 'talker', in NMEA jargon) and the 'listener' is simply a pair of wires. It's as robust and straightforward as the connection between a battery and a navigation light, but demands a little more care in how it is connected.

The first snag is usually identifying which terminal, or which of the various wires emerging from the plug supplied by the equipment manufacturers does which. Unfortunately, there is no standard colour coding, though the instruction manuals are usually helpful.

The key points to look for are that you must connect the output port of the talker to the input port of the listener, but you

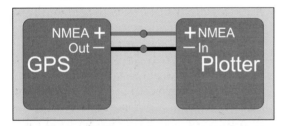

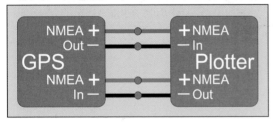

Fig 8 *The basic rules for making NMEA connections are to connect the output port of one device to the input port of the other, and connect positive to positive and negative to negative.*

connect positive to positive and negative to negative.

To achieve two-way communication between two pieces of equipment, requires four wires, in addition to the power supply to each of them. To save cabling, at the expense of making it more difficult to work out what is going on, however, some manufacturers make one wire serve as the negative connection for both input and output – and sometimes as the negative connection to the power supply, as well.

The next complication is that one talker can supply information to several listeners. Exactly how many varies, depending on the type of equipment you are talking about: most permanently-installed equipment can talk to four or five others, but a hand-held GPS may only manage two. The basics of the connections are exactly as they are for a single talker and listener, but it's important to make sure that there's only one talker in the system. If two devices are trying to talk simultaneously, their pulses of electricity will be superimposed on each other, so the listeners will receive a meaningless jumble.

There are two other requirements for a satisfactory NMEA 0183 interface. The first sounds obvious, but is easily neglected: make sure the talker is actually talking, and that it is sending NMEA 0183 data. Many GPS sets, for instance, leave the factory with their output ports switched off: you have to get into the 'setup' menu to switch them on. You can easily check, by connecting a voltmeter between the two wires that are supposed to be carrying the signal. You won't see individual pulses, because they are too fast for the voltmeter to react, but you should see a fluctuating voltage of somewhere between 0v and 5v if there's a NMEA signal present.

The other is that you must make sure that the listeners are expecting to receive data in the form that it is being sent. Some DSC radio controllers, for instance, look

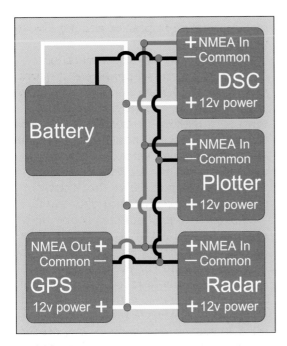

+ NMEA In
— Common
DSC
+ 12v power

Battery

+ NMEA In
— Common
Plotter
+ 12v power

NMEA Out +
Common —
GPS
12v power +

+ NMEA In
— Common
Radar
+ 12v power

Fig 9 *To save wire, the negative cores are often connected together to form a 'common ground': check with the instructions for each device.*

for position and time data in a sentence called RMC. If that doesn't happen to be amongst the sentences that your GPS is transmitting, the radio will listen in vain, oblivious to the fact that it could pick up the same information from any of several other sentences, such as the GLL sentence we looked at on page 23.

such as the GLL sentence we looked at on page 23.

The Five Rules of Interfacing

- Only one talker per circuit
- Output to input
- Positive to positive
- Check that the ports are open (ie switched on, and set to transmit or receive NMEA 0183)
- Check (in the manual) that the listener can accept the sentences that the talker is supplying

Opto-isolation

To us, the users, an NMEA 0183 connection can be regarded as nothing more than a pair of wires, but it's worth knowing that the NMEA specification requires a feature known as 'opto-isolation'. Hidden within the casing of the instrument, an opto-isolator uses a tiny LED to convert the incoming pulses of electricity into flashes of light, and a device called a phototransistor to convert the flashes back into pulses of electricity. The gap between the LED and the phototransistor is enough to isolate the electrical circuits of the listener from those of the talker.

Primarily intended to protect one instrument from electrical problems affecting the other, and to prevent stray currents passing through the interface if the two instruments were connected to different power supplies, opto-isolation also gives NMEA 0183 the flexibility to tolerate a wide range of voltages, and makes it almost immune to electrical interference.

4

What is GPS?

On 22 February 1978, the American government started a revolution in navigation by launching the first satellite of a system that would eventually provide accurate, continuously updated position information to anyone, anywhere on the Earth, by night or day and regardless of the weather.

By the end of that year, they had an experimental constellation of four Navstar GPS satellites in operation, and by 1985, there were another half dozen. The system wasn't declared fully operational until 1995, but by that time the price of civilian receivers had already fallen low enough for them to be becoming commonplace on small craft, with hand-held sets selling for as little as a couple of hundred pounds.

Now, GPS prices have fallen, accuracy has improved, and the system has a proven track record of accuracy and reliability.

Of course, this doesn't mean that there is 'no need to navigate'! The system can only tell you where you are, not whether you are where you should be, and individual receivers are still vulnerable to loss of power, loss of signal, and to 'finger trouble' or 'operator error'.

How it works

GPS uses a constellation of about two dozen satellites in orbit some 14,000km above the surface of the Earth (ie at an orbital radius of 20,200km). The number of satellites varies slightly, as old ones are taken out of service and as new ones are launched, but the general idea is that there are enough to ensure that a receiver any-

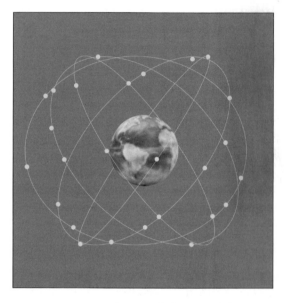

GPS uses a constellation of about two dozen satellites in orbit some 14,000km above the surface of the Earth.

where on the surface of the Earth should be able to receive the radio signals sent by at least four of them at a time.

Operating on microwave frequencies, ten times higher than marine VHF (1575.42MHz), each satellite transmits a signal which says, in effect, 'I am here...' and 'The time is now...'

Radio waves travel at a more or less constant speed of approximately 300,000km (162,000 nautical miles) per second[2], so if a

[2]In 1983, the Systeme Internationale defined the length of a metre as 1/299,792,458 the distance light travels in one second, so (by definition) the speed of light is 299,792,458 metres per second.

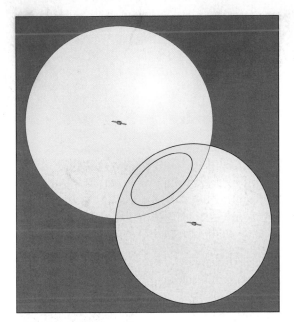

Fig 10 *When the receiver detects the signal from two satellites, it must be somewhere on the circle at which the two 'bubbles' meet.*

receiver detects the signal 0.07 seconds after it was sent, the receiver must be 21,000km from the satellite. This is called its 'pseudorange'. You can visualise the receiver as sitting somewhere on the surface of a huge, invisible bubble in space, whose centre is wherever the satellite was when it sent the signal, and whose radius is the distance the signal has travelled.

If the receiver also detects the signal from a second satellite, it can do the same thing again. It now 'knows' that it is on the surface of two such bubbles at once, which means that it must be somewhere on the circle at which the two bubbles meet. If it does the same thing with the signals from two more satellites, it can only be at the one particular position where all four bubbles intersect.

One big problem with this is that it all depends on very accurate timing. If the clock in the receiver is as little as a thousandth of a second fast, it will understate

the distance from each satellite by 300km, so the bubbles won't intersect neatly, at a single point. In terms that will be familiar to a traditional navigator, you won't get a pinpoint fix but a huge, three-dimensional cocked hat, shaped rather like a pyramid in space, and several hundred miles across.

For most practical purposes, we can safely assume that time of transmission was right, because each satellite carries several very accurate atomic clocks, which are compared with each other and with their counterparts in the other satellites by the GPS Master Control Station in Colorado. A civilian GPS set costing less than a hundred pounds cannot possibly be anything like as accurate. It can, however, adjust its own clock, tweaking the timing until the cocked hat is as small as possible.

The upshot of all this is that not only does GPS provide an accurate position; it also gives a very accurate indication of time, by effectively taking the consensus of a dozen or more atomic clocks.

GPS time

GPS time is not quite the same as Universal Time (UT). Although most GPS receivers show the time and date in a conventional format such as 31 Dec 2003 14:11:42, the **system** time is measured in weeks and seconds.

Another difference arises because there aren't really 24 hours in a day! The Earth is gradually slowing down so one complete spin now takes 24 hours and 2 milliseconds. To cope with this, once every eighteen months or so, we have a 'leap second' to put our clock time back in step with astronomical time. There is no reason, however, why GPS time needs to be synchronised with the apparent movement of the sun, so it does not use leap seconds at all. It was arbitrarily synchronised with UT on 6 January 1980, but (as at January 2004) is now 13 seconds ahead of it.

The satellites

You only need signals from four satellites to get a good fix, so you might assume that eight satellites would be enough – four of them might be on the other side of the Earth, but at least you should still be able to pick up signals from the other four. In practice, though, things aren't that simple: there would be times when five satellites would be below the horizon, and others when two satellites would be too close together to provide a good fix. So the original concept called for 18 satellites, plus three spares.

As time has gone by, expectations of GPS have grown, so there are about 28 satellites in the present constellation. The exact number varies slightly from time to time as old ones expire and new ones are launched. They are arranged in groups of four or five, with the members of each group chasing each other around one of six circular orbits 20,200km from the centre of the Earth.

The design of GPS satellites has also changed over the years, but all are quite substantial things. The original, experimental Block 1 satellites, for instance, weighed

760kg each, while the current Block 2Rs weigh just over two tonnes. They are nearly 2m square and 1.5m thick, with solar panels extending 5m on each side producing 2.5kW of power.

Satellite codes

Unlike the old radio direction finding (RDF) beacons or Decca stations, GPS satellites all transmit on the same frequency. This means we need some way to identify which signal is coming from which satellite. The signals are also very weak, which makes it difficult to pick them out against the background of random radio noise. Both problems are overcome by the use of 'pseudo random codes' (PRNs).

Each satellite has its own, specific PRN, consisting of over a thousand 'on' or 'off' pulses transmitted in a thousandth of a second. On its own, this crackle of data would

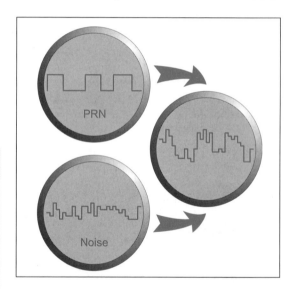

Fig 11 *Each satellite has its own, specific PRN, consisting of over a thousand 'on' or 'off' pulses transmitted in a thousandth of a second. On its own, this crackle of data would be lost amongst the random radio noise in space and in the atmosphere. The GPS receiver, however, produces an identical PRN, and feeds this into its own receiver.*

Two-dimensional fixing

A normal GPS fix uses the signals from at least four satellites to give a fix in three dimensions – latitude, longitude, and height. If the receiver knows its height, however, it can manage a two-dimensional fix with just three satellites. In effect, it uses the surface of the Earth in place of one of the pseudorange 'bubbles'. Unfortunately, the surface of the Earth is not a perfect sphere: sea level varies from place to place and from time to time, so a 2-D fix (based on three satellites plus the Earth) is never quite as accurate as a 3-D one (using four or more satellites).

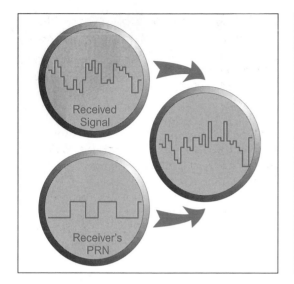

Fig 12 *At first, this merely adds to the confusion...*

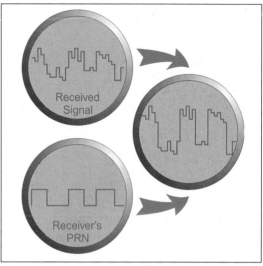

Fig 13 *...but when the receiver-generated code matches the code received from the satellite, they combine to produce a much stronger signal.*

be lost amongst the random radio noise in space and in the atmosphere. The GPS receiver, however, produces an identical PRN, and feeds this into its own receiver. At first, this merely adds to the confusion, but when the receiver-generated code matches the code received from the satellite, they combine to produce a much stronger signal.

Matching the satellite PRN with the receiver-generated PRN:

- is the basis for accurate timing;
- identifies a particular satellite's signal;
- allows low power GPS transmissions;
- makes it very difficult for anyone to 'jam' GPS, whether by accident or design.

Politics, codes, and accuracy

GPS was originally conceived as a military system. Even now, there are parts of the satellite signals which use a much faster, more complicated PRN. These 'P-code' signals are potentially more accurate and even better protected against jamming – but they are reserved for military use. In order to lock on to a P-code signal, however, a military receiver needs to know its approximate position. That is the real reason for the slower PRN code; it provides a Coarse Acquisition (CA) mode for the Precise (P-code) receiver.

To make GPS more cost-effective, the US Government decided to make the CA code signal available to civilians, believing that it would only be accurate to about 100m. It was soon found, however, that even CA code receivers were capable of getting positions accurate to about 15–20m.

To get back to its original designed specification, deliberate errors were built into the CA code signal, increasing the positioning error to about 100m. This policy was known as Selective Availability (SA). SA was 'set to zero' (in other words it was turned off) in May 2000. The US Government has said that it has no intention of reintroducing it, but is still capable of doing so.

Errors and accuracy

Even without Selective Availability (see page 29), GPS is subject to a number of genuine errors, including such things as satellite position errors, satellite clock errors, propagation errors (as the radio signal is bent by passing through the atmosphere) and various receiver errors.

▶▶	Error (metres) (per satellite)
Orbit error	2m
Satellite clock error	2m
Refraction (Ionosphere)	5m
Refraction (Troposphere)	1m
Multipath errors	1m
Receiver errors	<1m

Sometimes these add together, and sometimes they cancel each other out. Typically, though, the total range error for each satellite is in the order of 5–10m, due mostly to the refraction of the signal in the upper atmosphere.

Like the position lines which make up a visual fix, the angle at which the position spheres intersect also plays a part in the accuracy of the eventual fix. If the satellites are well spread, so the spheres intersect at a large angle, the fix is likely to be good – in GPS jargon, we say that the 'dilution of precision' (DOP) is small (see page 9). If the satellites are bunched together, or if the receiver's antenna is obstructed, the spheres may intersect at a much smaller angle, magnifying the effect of any errors.

> ▶▶ If the satellite signal error is 5m and the DOP is 3, the fix error is likely to be 5 x 3 = 15m
> If the satellite signal error is 5m and the DOP is 8, the fix error is likely to be 5 x 8 = 40m

In practice, at sea, a typical civilian GPS receiver is accurate to about 15–20m (at the 95% level of confidence).

> ▶▶ *You may know where you are to an accuracy of 15 metres, but do you know where the rocks are? Most charts were surveyed before such precise positioning systems existed.*

Improving the accuracy of GPS

For most navigational purposes, the accuracy of GPS is not really an issue. Even so, there are some users for whom an accuracy of 15m or so simply isn't good enough – some military applications, for instance, need better accuracy than this. So do surveyors, or even farmers, who nowadays use GPS to make sure they spread the right amounts of fertiliser and pesticides in the right bit of the right field!

One approach would be to get rid of the biggest source of error: atmospheric refraction. To make this possible, the satellites actually transmit their signals on two different frequencies, which are affected slightly differently by their passage through the atmosphere. By comparing the results obtained from the two sets of signals, a suitably equipped receiver can calculate the extent of the error, and compensate for it.

This, however, requires a considerably more sophisticated and expensive set than most users could justify.

It is relatively simple, on the other hand, to minimise the relatively small errors that arise at the receiver itself.

Multipath errors

Salt water is a good reflector of GPS signals, so a boat's GPS set at sea is likely to receive some signals that have been reflected from the surface of the sea, which will have travelled further than those that have arrived direct from the satellite. This could confuse its range calculations, causing

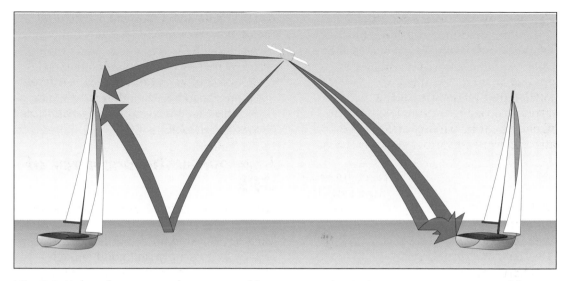

Fig 14 *Multipath errors can be minimised by mounting the GPS antenna as* LOW *as possible.*

multipath errors. Multipath errors can be minimised by mounting the GPS antenna as LOW as possible.

Receiver noise

Random radio 'noise', similar to the hissing and crackling you hear on a VHF radio when the squelch is set too low, can upset the GPS set's ability to pick out and accurately time the incoming satellite signal. Some of this noise is produced by the set itself, so there is not much the user can do about it. We can, however, help by making sure that the GPS is not subjected to unnecessary radio interference.

Fortunately, the most difficult sources of radio interference, such as fluorescent lights and engine electrics, don't seem to have much effect on GPS, because they are at a much lower frequency. The chief offenders are radar, radar target enhancers, satellite communications equipment, and – to a lesser extent – some mobile telephones. The powerful transmissions from a radar, in particular, can completely deafen the GPS to the very weak signals it is trying to detect.

Interference can be minimised by mount-ing a GPS antenna well outside the beam of a radar scanner, at least a metre away from a satcom or radar target enhancer, and by keeping its cable well clear of any other antenna cable.

Differential GPS (DGPS)

If you know about an error, you are well on the way to correcting for it. Unfortunately, most of the errors that afflict GPS fluctuate quickly and unpredictably, so the only way to get up-to-the-second corrections is by radio, from fixed reference stations ashore.

Suitably-equipped GPS sets, often described as 'differential ready', can apply the corrections received from reference stations to achieve fixes that are roughly twice as accurate as those from stand-alone GPS – about 7–8m.

In principle, almost any radio frequency could be used to broadcast differential corrections, but in practice, for marine use, it is generally about the same as the now-obsolete Radio Direction Finding beacons: about 300kHz. This gives good, cost-effective coverage of coastal waters and several hundred miles offshore, but is so much lower than the frequency used by GPS itself that it needs a completely separate antenna and receiver, known as a **Differential Beacon Receiver**.

To receive DGPS, you need a completely separate antenna and receiver, known as a Differential Beacon Receiver.

Satellite differential GPS

An alternative would be to use satellites to broadcast the differential corrections. This has the advantage of covering wide areas without needing to use low frequencies so the receiver can be built into a GPS set and

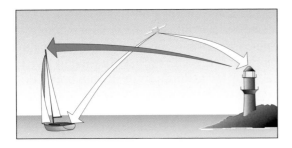

Fig 15 *Differential GPS relies on reference stations ashore, which monitor the satellite signals, and broadcast corrections.*

use the same antenna. Because the area that can be covered by a single communications satellite is very much bigger than the area covered by a shore-based differential reference station, several reference stations are linked together, to gather information from more satellites, and to pool their information. Satellite differential increases the accuracy of GPS to about 3–4m.

There are three satellite differential systems:

Wide Area Augmentation System (WAAS) was declared operational on 10 July 2003. It uses 25 ground-based reference stations and two communications satellites to cover the whole of North America up to about 70°N, and adjoining waters of the Atlantic and Pacific.

The European Geostationary Navigational Overlay System (EGNOS) is expected to be declared operational during 2005. It will have 31 reference stations, mostly in Europe, but with others in North and South America, Africa, Iceland and Malaysia, and will use three communications satellites to cover the whole of the Atlantic and Indian Oceans as well as Europe and Africa.

MTSAT Satellite-based Augmentation System (MSAS) is a satellite differential system to be carried on board the Japanese Multifunction Transport Satellite (MTSAT), alongside its weather forecasting and air traffic control functions. The first MTSAT was destroyed on launching but its replacement should be launched during 2005. It will use at least eight reference stations in Hawaii and Australia as well as Japan, and should cover most of the area missed by WAAS and EGNOS.

Why DGPS?

In the days before SA was switched off, GPS simply wasn't accurate enough for many users – such as divers and fishermen. Now, GPS by itself is accurate enough for most purposes.

DGPS and SDGPS, however, are still useful, because they provide an immediate warning and correction if the GPS signal is disrupted by jamming or 'spoofing'. SDGPS, in particular, provides this added safeguard at very little extra cost to the user, so is fast becoming standard on all but the cheapest GPS sets.

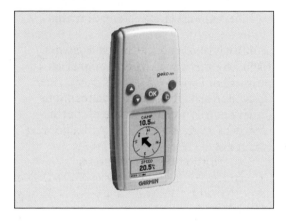

Satellite differential capability is now virtually standard, even in low-budget hand-helds.

Other satnavs

GPS is not the only satellite navigation system.

Glonass was set up by the Soviet Union at about the same time as the USA launched GPS. It works in a similar way, and is theoretically capable of similar accuracy, but was plagued by reliability problems. The Russian Federation has declared that it intends to restore Glonass to full operation by 2006, and in January 2004 had eight operational satellites in orbit.

Galileo is the European counterpart to GPS. It is a much newer system, with the advantage of nearly 30 years of advances in technology. An experimental satellite is due to be launched by the end of 2005 and the system is expected to be declared operational with 30 satellites in 2008.

5

Using GPS

Most GPS receivers have similar features and controls, but the way those controls are actually operated varies widely between models. Expect to have to read and refer back to the instructions until you become thoroughly familiar with your particular model.

Initialising

When a GPS set is brand new, or has been stored for a long period without power, or has been moved a long distance whilst

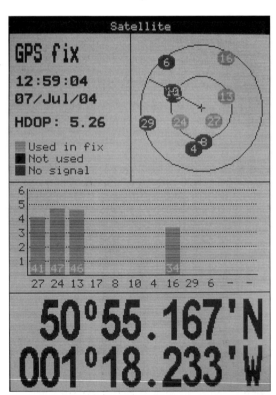

switched off, it has no idea which satellites it can expect to 'see', so it will take time to search and lock on to their PRN codes. Each satellite transmits data about the position of all the other satellites (called the ephemeris), but it takes 12½ minutes to download the whole sequence, so it may well take a quarter of an hour or so for a brand new GPS receiver to get its first 'fix'.

- You can usually reduce the time to first fix by telling the GPS set the time, date, and approximate position.

- Most sets offer a 'satellite status' display which will show which satellites have been located and locked on: this may also indicate where the satellites are and which others the set is expecting to 'see'.

- So long as the GPS has reasonably up to date data stored in its memory, subsequent fixes will be very much quicker: typically within 2 minutes of switching on, and sometimes within a few seconds.

Set-up options

There is usually plenty to do while you are waiting for the first fix from a new GPS, because most sets can be customised to suit individual preferences. Some of these set-up features are cosmetic, such as whether the keys 'beep' when they are pressed, but some are much more important.

Most GPS sets include a satellite status display, showing which satellites the set expects to 'see' and which it is actually using.

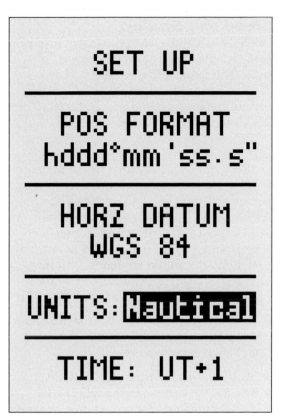

```
        SET UP
─────────────────
      POS FORMAT
     hddd°mm'ss.s"
─────────────────
      HORZ DATUM
       WGS 84
─────────────────
    UNITS:Nautical
─────────────────
      TIME: UT+1
```

Fig 16 *A set-up menu allows you to make essential choices, such as the way position is expressed, the units you use, and the time zone.*

specific units for different measurements (such as distances in nautical miles but heights in metres). Be warned, though, that as the number of non-marine users of GPS has increased, many GPS sets now leave the factory pre-set to show distances in statute miles or kilometres and speeds in mph or kph.

Position
Position can be expressed in several different **formats**, including degrees, minutes, and hundredths (most useful for general marine navigation); degrees, minutes and thousandths; degrees, minutes and seconds; or a variety of grids such as Ordnance Survey.

- Make sure you select the right **datum** for the chart you are using (see page 6).

- Remember to change the datum when you change charts.

Direction
Direction is usually given in degrees relative to True north, but many GPS sets can show magnetic bearings, either using automatically calculated variation, or using a figure entered manually. Some also offer alternative units, such as mils, grads or gons!

Alarms
Most GPS sets offer a variety of alarms, such as a **waypoint alarm** and **cross track alarm,** which can be set to warn you as you approach a waypoint (see page 40) or stray off your intended track (see page 40).

Basic displays

As graphic displays become more common, numerical displays are increasingly regarded as less important, and on some of the latest models, you may have to search the set-up options quite carefully to get latitude and longitude to appear on the

Time
Time and date are derived from the GPS satellites, usually adjusted to UTC (Greenwich Mean Time). You cannot 'correct' them, but you can usually choose the way in which dates are shown (day/month/ year or month/day/year), whether times are in 12-hour or 24-hour format, and whether a correction is applied for time zones or daylight-saving time.

Units
Units of measurement may be selected in general terms such as 'nautical', 'statute', 'metric' or you may be able to select

screen at all! All marine GPS sets, however, can show position, time, and track (course and speed over the ground).

Position, time and date

Make sure your GPS is set up to display position and time:

- In the right format (eg lat and long, rather than grid references)

- In the right units (eg degrees, minutes, and hundredths)

- Positions referred to the correct datum and time referred to the correct time zone.

Don't be afraid to use the set-up menu to change anything that does not suit you.

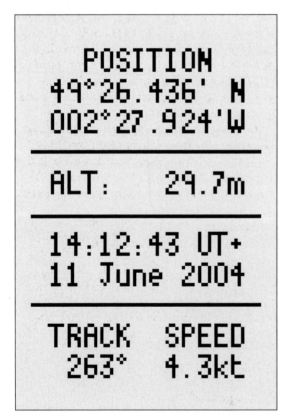

Fig 17 *The most basic display can be expected to show position, time, and date.*

Speed and direction

A GPS set is not a compass (though some models have an electronic compass built in) so the speed and direction it shows refer to your movement over the ground, not to the direction the boat is pointing or your speed through the water.

Different models use different terminology; you may well come across:

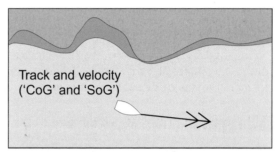

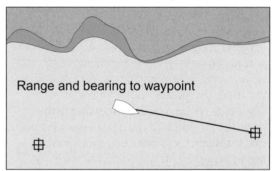

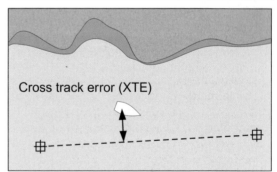

Fig 18 *As well as position, a GPS set can be expected to show your speed and direction of movement, the direction and distance to a pre-planned waypoint, and your cross track error.*

- Course and Speed (or CRS, SPD)

- Heading and Speed (HDG and SPD)

- Track and Velocity (or TRK, VEL)

- Course and Speed over Ground (CoG and SoG)

If you're not moving, the velocity will fluctuate close to zero, but the track will show apparently random changes. The accuracy of both increases as speed increases.

Some GPS sets have a 'damping' or 'averaging' facility: this reduces the fluctuations, but makes the set slower to respond to real changes of direction and speed.

Waypoint navigation

Most GPS sets are able to store a number of 'waypoints' and 'routes'.

A 'waypoint' is simply a position. The original idea was that it was a point somewhere along your way, but there is no reason why you should not use waypoints for other purposes. You could use a waypoint to mark a position that you specifically want to avoid, or one that you do not want to move away from (such as an anchorage), or even an arbitrary reference point.

A 'route', in this context, is a planned journey, made up of a series of one or more straight lines between waypoints.

- Waypoints are sometimes referred to as 'marks', 'landmarks', or 'routepoints'.

- Procedures for creating and storing waypoints vary so **read the instructions**!

- One of the most useful waypoints is the fairway buoy or harbour entrance to your home port.

'Go To'

The simplest kind of route has just one waypoint – your destination. Many GPS sets have a button marked 'Go To' which allows you to set up this type of route particularly easily: you just press the 'Go To' button then select the target waypoint from a list on the screen. The GPS set will then guide you to that waypoint by supplying some (or all) of the following information:

Distance to Waypoint = the distance you have to go to reach the waypoint from your present position.

Bearing to Waypoint = the direction to the waypoint from your present position.

Time To Go or Estimated Time En Route (ETE) or Estimated Time of Arrival (ETA) assuming you maintain your present speed.

The law says...

Tempting as it may be to set off into the sunset, the reality is that every trip, no matter how short, involves some degree of planning. Skimp on the preparation, and you may well find yourself fighting a foul tide, or arriving to find the harbour entrance blocked by a lock that isn't due to open for another six hours...or worse.

To these practical considerations has now been added a legal obligation under which the master of any vessel from a windsurfer upwards is required to 'ensure that the intended voyage has been planned using the appropriate nautical charts and publications for the area concerned'. In particular, the Maritime and Coastguard Agency say that the plan should consider:
- an up to date weather forecast;
- tidal predictions;
- the limitations of the boat and crew;
- navigational dangers;
- a contingency plan;
- details left with a responsible person ashore.

Cross Track Error (often abbreviated to XTE) = the distance you've strayed from the straight line route between your starting position and the waypoint.

Graphic displays such as the 'compass' or 'rolling road' present much the same information but in a form that is more accessible to inexperienced navigators.

Route navigation

The law doesn't actually say that you need to have an intended track drawn on the chart. For anyone navigating by traditional methods, particularly in a sailing yacht, it seems pretty pointless to do so: it's better to set off in the right general direction, monitor progress by whatever means you can, and adapt the course you are steering to suit the situation as the passage progresses.

To make best use of GPS, however, we have to break with tradition, because drawing an intended track onto the chart is an essential step towards what is now widely known as 'waypoint navigation'.

It's a very useful technique, though the name is somewhat unfortunate because it puts the cart before the horse by suggesting that a route is made up by drawing lines from one waypoint to the next. That impression is reinforced by published lists of waypoints, in almanacs and pilot books, and by GPS sets sold with a standard 'library' of waypoints already stored in their memories.

Passage planning, however, is not a matter of joining the dots between a succession of more or less arbitrary waypoints! *Let the route dictate the position of the waypoints, not vice versa.*

One useful idea is to take a pencil and draw a freehand sketch on the chart of what you think will be the best route around major turning points, such as headlands. Then, look for places on or close to your freehand route at which it will be particularly easy to check your position by non-electronic methods, such as where a transit crosses a contour line.

These are the prime contenders for waypoints, so try joining them up with neat,

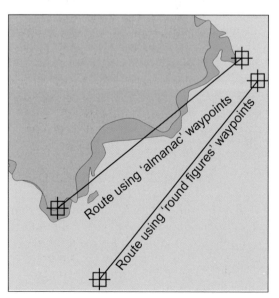
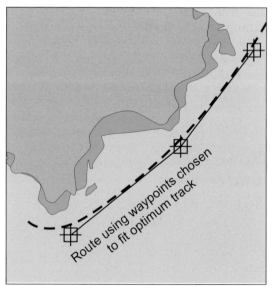

Fig 19 *Let the route dictate the position of the waypoints, not vice versa.*

ruled lines, before ruling the longer straight lines that will represent the longer legs of the passage, between headands. By doing it this way, you avoid the Scylla and Charybdis temptations of either cutting the corner too fine (to save yourself the trouble of putting in an extra waypoint) or adding extra miles to the trip just to go to a waypoint whose only attraction is that its latitude and longitude are nice round numbers!

It's also a very good idea to measure the distance and direction to each waypoint from the one before, and to make a note of it on the chart. Of course this helps you work out how long the passage is, even though the lines drawn on the chart may not bear much resemblance to where you actually go, but it does two much more important things.

First, it serves as a double check that you've 'entered' the waypoints into the GPS accurately. If the chart says two waypoints are 8 miles apart, on a bearing of 290, and the GPS says that they are 58 miles apart, bearing 188, it is pretty obvious that there is something wrong with one of them. This is exactly the sort of thing that happens when you accidentally key in a latitude that is exactly one degree wrong. Of course, if you can honestly claim never to have dialled a wrong number, you need not bother!

Secondly, it paves the way for another useful technique, known as a ladder plot (see page 43).

Routes and waypoints under way

Real navigation, of course, doesn't stop when you've drawn a line across a chart: the whole point of the exercise is to get the boat to move across the real world more or less in accordance with the paper plan!

Starting error

The first problem can arise before you've

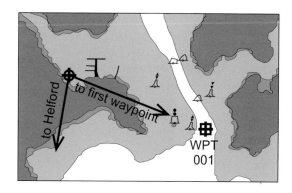

Fig 20 *So-called 'starting error' isn't really an error at all: the GPS will quite accurately show the bearing to your next waypoint or destination, even if you can't actually go that way.*

even left the mooring or marina, when the GPS shows a direction to your first waypoint that is clearly impractical, such as straight across a harbour wall. This is sometimes called 'starting error', for obvious reasons. It's rather unfair to call it an 'error', though.

It arises because human navigators tend to take it for granted that the helmsman would be steering by eye for at least the first few metres of the trip, and put the first waypoint just outside the marina, or at the mouth of the river, or whatever.

There are good reasons for doing this but of course the GPS cannot be expected to 'know' that there are pontoons or riverbanks in the way and will quite correctly indicate the distance and direction to the first waypoint.

This may seem like a statement of the obvious, but it's worth bearing in mind because it is important to know where your route begins and ends. Leaving Falmouth for a passage to Helford, for instance, it may be perfectly reasonable for the first waypoint to be at the harbour entrance, and it is pretty obvious, in the marina, that we can't go straight to it (see Fig 20). As soon as we are clear of the marina and the commercial docks, however, the helmsman will certainly want to know whether it is safe to head straight for Waypoint 1, or whether the navigator assumed that he would be following the buoyed channel.

Cross track error

Everyone knows that the shortest distance between two points is a straight line, so the cross track error display, showing how far we have strayed from the straight line track to the next waypoint, is especially useful. Novice helmsmen, in particular, often find it much easier to steer accurately by using the 'rolling road' display of a GPS than by referring to a traditional compass. It has its drawbacks, though.

A 'rolling road' display is popular with novice helmsmen. Steering to stay 'on the road' is much more efficient than trying to keep the cross track error at zero.

The first drawback is that there is a natural tendency for the helmsman to want to keep the cross track error to zero, and to overcompensate for very small errors. The result is that he (or she) finds himself steering a zig-zag course.

It's similar, in some ways, to what would happen if you tried to steer a car by hanging out of the window to look at distance between the front wheel and the white line! Of course, you wouldn't dream of driving like that: you'd be much more likely to look forwards, and aim to stay between the white line and the kerb. The same idea works with the cross track error display. Set yourself a reasonable limit, such as a quarter of a mile, and stay within it by watching for trends in the cross track error display using occasional small alterations of course to stay within your limits.

The second problem with the cross track error display is that the GPS knows nothing about tidal streams. Steering to stay on track may be a reasonable tactic on a short passage, but if the trip is likely to last more than an hour or so you will almost certainly be dealing with a changing tidal stream. Staying on track in a cross-tide is a very inefficient way of doing things, especially if your boat is slow or the tide is strong.

Waypoint arrival

Almost all GPS sets include a 'waypoint arrival alarm', to warn you that you are approaching a waypoint. There's usually some facility, somewhere in the set-up menu (don't be afraid to refer to the instructions!), to set up the waypoint arrival alarm to suit your own, particular requirements. At its simplest, this may be simply an 'arrival distance': if you set it to 200m, the alarm will sound when you are 200m from the waypoint, regardless of whether it is ahead of you or abeam.

More importantly, in some respects, the waypoint arrival alarm tells the GPS set or

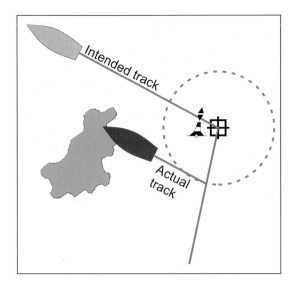

Fig 21 *Altering course when the waypoint arrival alarm sounds can mean that you end up following a different track than you intended.*

plotter when to turn its attention to the next waypoint in the route.

More sophisticated versions will trigger when you cross the next leg of the route, or when you are as close to the waypoint as you will ever get without altering course, or when you cross the line that bisects the angle between your present track and the next leg of the route. All these options have been developed in order to help you, but you do need to think quite carefully about the implications of using each one. *If in doubt, revert to the simple, range-based arrival alarm.*

Even the range-based arrival alarm needs to be treated with a certain amount of care, particularly if it is used to trigger a course change on an autopilot:

• It is never worth setting the alarm distance to less than the accuracy of the navigation system, and seldom worth setting it to less than about 0.1 miles (roughly 200m), because if you don't pass close

enough to the waypoint to trigger the alarm, the GPS will not switch to the next leg of the route.

• If you set a large alarm distance, be aware of the fact that the alarm will be triggered when you are some distance away from the waypoint, so if you alter course as soon as the alarm sounds, you may well be a long way off your intended track.

▶▶ *When you arrive at a waypoint, check it by eye or by echo sounder if possible: if you have chosen your own waypoints, this should be easy!*

Using waypoints to monitor position

'Knowing your position' is no use unless you can relate it to the world around you, usually by plotting it on a chart.

Fig 22 *Plotting a fix based on the range and bearing to a waypoint is often quicker and easier than by latitude and longitude, but remember that GPS shows the bearing TO the waypoint, not FROM it. Add or subtract 180 degrees to convert.*

The obvious way to plot a GPS position is by using the latitude and longitude display, but the waypoint facility offers several alternatives, which may prove much quicker and easier, and therefore more reliable.

▸▸ *Always try to keep a regularly updated record of your position, either on the chart or in a log book or notepad.*

Range and bearing of waypoint
The GPS may indicate the range and bearing to the next waypoint.

If, for instance, you are 230°, 1.9 miles from the waypoint, you know you are on a line drawn in the direction 230°, passing through the waypoint. At the same time, you are on a circle with a radius of 1.9 miles, with the waypoint at its centre.

This method is good for short distances but the effect of errors increases with distance: for every 6 miles, a one degree error amounts to a 185m error in position.

Waypoint web
A variation on this theme is particularly useful when day-sailing, or when approaching your home port, because although it takes quite a lot of preparation, it virtually eliminates chart-work under way.

Draw your own compass rose around a favourite waypoint (such as the fairway

buoy or harbour entrance of your home port) and add range rings to produce a pattern rather like a spider's web. The range and bearing, from the GPS, will allow you to find your position within the web with surprising accuracy with no further plotting whatsoever.

Range and bearing of a compass rose
This uses exactly the same principle, except that it uses the centre of a compass rose, printed on the chart, as a waypoint. Of course it is highly unlikely that you will

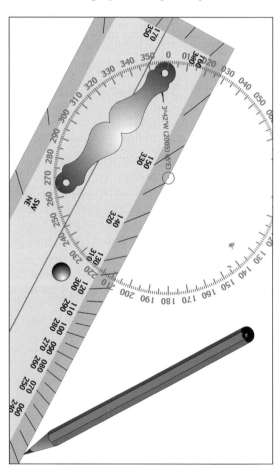

Fig 24 *The centre of a compass rose can be stored as a reference point to make plotting fixes easier.*

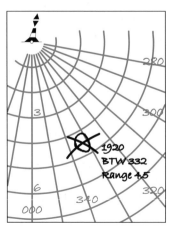

Fig 23
A spider's web pattern of ranges and bearings drawn around a landmark is a useful way to speed up the plotting process.

ever want to go to the centre of the compass rose, but it makes the chartwork very much easier: just lay any straight edge across the compass rose to plot the bearing!

Cross track error ladder

Positions based on bearing become inaccurate over long distances, and a big 'web' is tedious to construct.

You can use distance to waypoint and cross track error (XTE) to achieve a similar result, however, by drawing a 'ladder' pattern on the chart, based on your intended track. It takes a little more preparation, but once on passage, the chartwork is cut to a minimum: the distance to waypoint shows which 'rung' of the ladder you are on, and the XTE display shows where you are relative to the centreline and the 'uprights'.

The accuracy of a ladder plot is good so long as the distance to waypoint is significantly bigger than the cross track error; at ranges of less than about 5–6 miles, it is worth considering changing to a plot based on bearings.

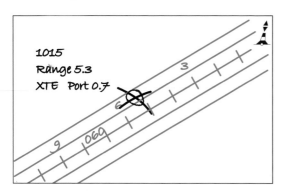

Fig 25 *On passage, a 'ladder' drawn on the chart allows you to keep track of your position by referring to the cross track error and distance to go.*

Upwind sailing

Cruising sailors seldom find themselves faced with a true beat to windward, in which their destination is directly upwind. More often, it's a slightly skewed beat, in which you are destined to spend more time on one tack than on the other.

Given plenty of open water, and ignoring the effects of tide, most people would probably set off on the tack which took them most directly towards their destination. That much, at least, is almost instinctive, and instinct, in this case, is perfectly correct. It is much more difficult to decide when is the best moment to tack.

The 'cone' and 'corridor' strategies are both intended to help you hedge your bets, by helping you avoid the temptation to stay on one tack for so long that you risk being caught out by an unexpected windshift.

The cone strategy

Navigating on paper, you would prepare for the cone strategy by drawing a line on the chart, extending directly downwind of the intended destination, with two more lines – one on each side of the downwind line – diverging from it so as to form a cone or funnel-shaped approach. The idea is that you should stay within the funnel, so that you are always more or less downwind of your destination, which means that any windshift will make things better rather than worse.

Exactly how wide the cone should be is very much a matter of individual preference. A very narrow cone, perhaps as little as 10 degrees wide, offers good protection against windshifts, but involves a lot of short-tacking, whereas a wide cone, maybe 60 degrees across, leaves you at much greater risk of being caught out. A typical compromise is to make the edges diverge from the downwind line at about 15 or 20 degrees, to give a cone some 30 or 40 degrees across.

Using GPS, the cone strategy requires no such preparation; you simply store your destination as a waypoint, and tell the GPS that you want to 'Go To' it.

Then, note the direction of the wind, and add or subtract 180 degrees to find what the bearing to waypoint would be if you were directly downwind of it.

Finally, add *and* subtract the angle of your cone from this, to find the edges of the cone, and tack whenever the bearing to waypoint display corresponds with either of these edges.

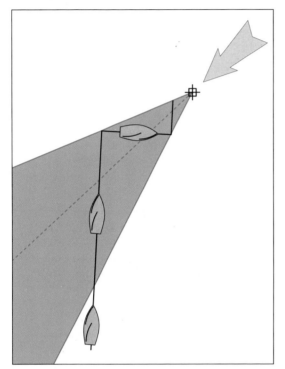

Fig 26 *When beating upwind, a sailing yacht can be kept in the 'cone' approach to a waypoint by monitoring the bearing to waypoint display.*

▶▶ **For example:**
Suppose the wind is SSW, and we want to use a 40 degree cone:
SSW = 202°
So the bearing to waypoint from anywhere on the downwind line is 202°
A 40° cone requires 20° each side of downwind, ie 202°+20°=222° and

202°−20°=182°
Tack whenever the bearing to waypoint reaches 182° or 222°

The corridor strategy

One problem with the cone strategy is that at the start of a long passage, the tacks may be very long. A few hours later, when the crew are starting to get tired, the tacks come thick and fast. An alternative is the corridor strategy. The principle for this is the same as the cone strategy, except that the waypoint is approached through a parallel-sided corridor instead of a tapering funnel.

On paper, the preparation of a corridor is very similar to the cone; you start by drawing a line on the chart extending directly downwind of the intended destination, then add another line, parallel to it on

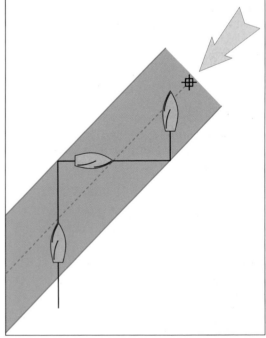

Fig 27 *An alternative to the cone approach is to stay in the downwind 'corridor': here it is the cross track error which tells you when to tack.*

each side to mark the edges of the corridor.

The similarity to a cross-track ladder is obvious. The big difference is that you need to set the cross track error to zero the first time you cross the downwind line. How you achieve this in practice varies from one set to another: it may, for instance, involve watching the bearing to waypoint display until it is exactly 180° more or less than the wind direction, before temporarily abandoning any route navigation in favour of a new 'Go To' route towards the up-wind waypoint.

Again, the width of the corridor is a matter of personal preference: a 2-mile corridor, for instance, would involve tack-ing whenever the cross track error display reached 1.0 mile. Just as with the cone strategy, a narrow corridor offers greater reassurance, but involves more work. Whatever you decide, the important thing is to stick to it, and not to give into the temptation to 'hold on to this tack until after we've had a cup of tea'.

Lay lines

Perhaps the most useful of all upwind tac-tics involves what are known as lay lines, which represent the ground track of the boat if she is just capable of reaching the windward waypoint without tacking. The significance of this is that the lay line shows you when to tack if you are to avoid beating any further to windward than necessary.

For the traditional navigator, working out lay lines was a somewhat tedious busi-ness, so most cruising yachtsmen probably didn't bother – we'd tack when the mark was abeam, give or take a bit depending on the tide and our confidence.

GPS, however, makes it easy. Assuming the wind and tidal stream are more or less constant – which shouldn't be too unrealis-tic if you are in a reasonably typical sailing cruiser and within about an hour of the waypoint – simply note your ground track

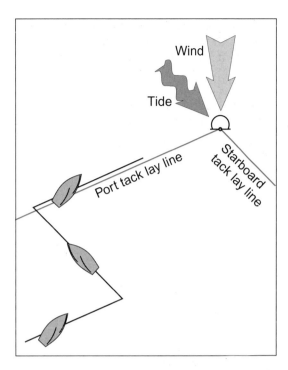

Fig 28 *The lay line is the line from which it is possible to reach the waypoint without tacking. Note your track (CoG) on each tack, and tack when the bearing to waypoint matches the CoG achieved on the opposite tack.*

(CoG or CMG) when you are close-hauled on each tack. Then watch the bearing to waypoint display, and tack when the bear-ing to waypoint matches either of the close-hauled ground tracks.

GPS pilotage

Many older text books insist that GPS should never be used for pilotage. That was certainly true in the days when the accuracy of the system was deliberately degraded to 100m, but now that a typical civilian GPS set is capable of giving fixes accurate to about 15m, there is no real rea-son to write it off in quite the same way!

In most cases, a GPS position will be much more accurate and reliable than any

Key waypoint tips

- Let your route dictate the position of your waypoints, not vice versa.
- If possible, position waypoints where your arrival can easily be checked by traditional methods – such as on a transit or contour.
- Never use a waypoint from a book or magazine without checking it on the chart; it may involve a dangerous short cut or an unnecessary detour.
- Check the legs of the route between waypoints, not just the waypoints themselves. Does the route pass dangerously close to

- a hazard? If so, consider moving a waypoint or inserting an extra one.
- It's easier to enter the wrong latitude and longitude for a waypoint than it is to dial a wrong telephone number. If possible, get someone else to check your figures.
- Once the waypoints have been stored in the GPS, use the 'route review' facility to check that the range and bearing of each waypoint from the one before corresponds with the distances and directions measured on the chart.

other pilotage technique except, perhaps, a transit. If anything, the problem is that it may be more accurate than the chart, so you may run aground because the rock or sandbank is in the wrong place, rather than because you are! The practical effect, of course, is the same, so GPS still needs to be used with caution in close-quarters, pilotage waters.

Clearing bearings

The illustration shows a bay fringed by rocky shallows.

The classic, traditional navigator's way of dealing with this situation would be a technique known as clearing bearings. This involves noting what the bearing of a conspicuous landmark would be if you were just on the limit of the safe water. This is the clearing bearing. Then as you approach the hazard, you use a hand-bearing compass to monitor the actual bearing, to make sure that you stay on the safe side of the invisible line.

A typical example is shown in Fig 29,

where the approaches to a river entrance are fringed by rocky shallows. Fortunately, there's a church on the hillside, whose

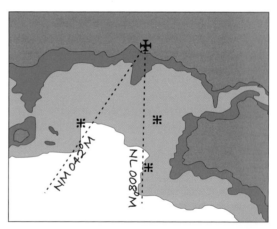

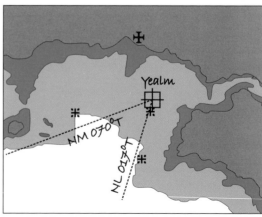

Fig 29 *Visual clearing bearings (above) use the visual bearing of a landmark to stay in a funnel-shaped approach. GPS clearing bearings are just the same, except that you can use any waypoint instead of a visible landmark.*

bearing would be 008° if we were passing just clear of the rocks on the eastern side of the bay. This means that so long as the bearing of the church is bigger than 008°, we must be in the safe water to the west of the rocks.

Similarly, if we were just squeezing past the rocks on the western side of the bay, the bearing of the church would be 042°, so by keeping the bearing less than that, we can be sure of passing safely to the east of the rocks.

We could achieve much the same thing by storing the position of the church as a 'Go To' waypoint in the GPS, and monitoring its bearing by watching the bearing to waypoint display – but there isn't much point! One of the beauties of GPS is that we can use waypoints as electronic landmarks, and put them wherever we want.

In this particular case (Fig 29), our route finishes at a waypoint called 'Yealm', which is well-placed to serve as a reference point for the clearing lines. The only preparation required is to make a note of the safe clearing bearings.

XTE limit

A variation on the idea of clearing bearings is to make sure you know the maximum cross track error you can accept at different stages of a passage. This is particularly useful, and important, when your planned route passes close to a hazard, as seen in Fig 30.

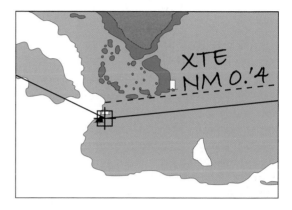

Fig 30 *Knowing the acceptable limits of cross track error stops you from straying into danger, but means you don't worry if you drift a few metres off your intended track.*

6

Chart plotters

A chart plotter is an electronic device on which your present position – usually from a GPS receiver – is displayed as a marker on an electronic chart.

That simple definition, however, covers a vast and growing range of products, including dedicated equipment designed for use on commercial ships, with customised control panels and displays that are the size of a large-screen television, through personal computers running specialised software, to hand-held devices with monochrome screens only a few centimetres wide. In some, the position information comes from a GPS built into the plotter itself, while other chart plotters have to be interfaced to a separate GPS receiver.

To make some sense of this complex market, it is useful to subdivide.

ECDIS or ECS?

The abbreviation ECDIS stands for Electronic Chart Display and Information System; it refers to any chart plotting system that meets the international standards laid down for electronic chart plotters on commercial vessels that are required, by law, to carry official government charts.

ECS stands for Electronic Charting System. Strictly speaking, of course, it includes ECDIS, but in practice it tends to be used to mean chart plotting systems that

The legal position

The Safety of Life at Sea Convention requires large commercial vessels (so-called 'convention ships') to carry approved navigational charts. This requirement can be met by approved ECDIS systems displaying vector charts (called Electronic Navigational Charts, or ENCs), so long as there is a back-up system available.

Raster charts (called RNCs) may be used in areas where ENCs are not available, but only with paper charts as a back-up.

The full weight of SOLAS regulations do not apply to small craft. In particular, we're not required to carry 'approved' charts. We are, however, required to plan our passage using 'appropriate' charts. This requirement can be met by using paper charts from non-government sources, such as Imray or Stanfords, or by using electronic charts from non-government sources such as C-Map or Navionics (known as ECs).

The interpretation of this legislation has not yet been tested in court, but it makes sense to carry some form of back-up – and it is not unreasonable to believe that the courts might assume that a system using raster charts should be backed up by paper charts.

The back-up folio of paper charts need not be as extensive as would be required if you were navigating entirely by traditional methods. You could, for instance, carry a small scale paper chart of your cruising area with detailed charts only of a few major ports, rather than of every harbour you intended to visit.

do *not* meet ECDIS requirements, including the overwhelming majority of dedicated chart plotters and PC-based navigation systems used on small craft.

Hardware or software?

All electronic charting systems include both hardware and software (see Chapter 3), but the terms 'hardware' and 'software' are a convenient shorthand to separate chart plotting software that is designed to be run on almost any personal computer from systems that consist of dedicated chart plotting hardware in which pre-loaded software is an integral part of the package.

Raster or vector?

The third way of classifying chart plotters is on the basis of the kind of charts they use: raster or vector. Almost all hardware plotters use vector charts, while most software plotters use raster charts, though the balance is shifting in favour of vector charts.

Raster charts

A raster chart can be summed up as a photograph or facsimile of a paper chart. The paper chart – or the four mylar films used to produce the plates from which it was

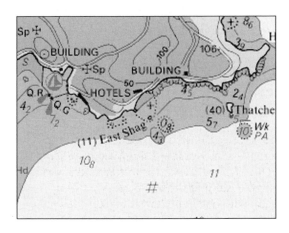

A raster chart looks just like a paper chart.

printed – is scanned by something like a giant fax machine.

A fax machine scans backwards and forwards across a document, breaking it up into several lines, in which each line is made up of a number of pixels (picture elements). It then transmits the position and colour of each pixel down the telephone line as a sequence of very rapid pulses. We hear this as a crackling or hissing sound, but another fax machine can produce a copy of the original document by reassembling the pixels. It prints them out, line by line, with each pixel coloured light or dark according to the information it receives.

A chart scanner does just the same thing, except that instead of sending the information as pulses transmitted through a telephone line, it stores the colour and position of each pixel.

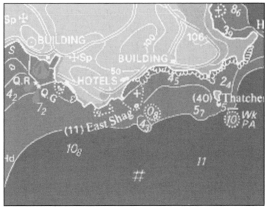

Some software can change the colours of a raster chart, to make it less dazzling at night.

Raster charts look exactly like the paper originals. Nothing is added or taken away, although those that are scanned from films (including the British Admiralty ARCS charts) can have their colours changed by the plotting software, to reduce glare at night.

ARCS charts

Although there are a few non-government sources of raster charts, by far the best-known is the Admiralty Raster Chart System (ARCS), produced by the UK Hydrographic Office, whose complete series of over 3000 individual charts is contained in 10 compact discs. When you 'buy' a folio of electronic charts, however, you won't be able to access all the charts which may be stored on your particular disc, because what you have bought is a licence to use a certain number of charts, with access to them controlled by a security code.

Updates to raster charts are achieved by adding replacement 'patches' or 'tiles' to the basic chart. You buy the updates by subscribing to an annual or quarterly update service, which supplies another compact disc containing all the relevant updates. The chart plotting software then superimposes the image of the updated portion of the chart onto the image of the original chart.

Changing charts

Because a raster chart is an image of the original paper chart, it is best viewed at the same scale as the original. It is possible to zoom in or out, just as it is possible to zoom in or out of a digital photograph displayed on a computer, but it is only practical to do so to a limited extent.

The effect is very much the same as looking at a paper chart through a magnifying glass or through the wrong end of a pair of binoculars. Zooming in makes things look bigger, without adding any extra information, while zooming out shows a bigger area, but reduces the size of text and symbols to such an extent that they may become unreadable.

You can quite sensibly zoom out in order to get an overview or zoom in to make it easier to see fine detail, but you should never overdo it, and certainly not try to use a coastal chart for pilotage. In other words,

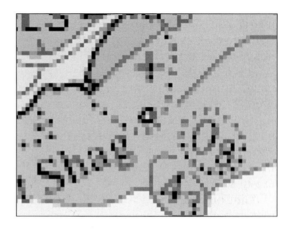

Zooming in on a raster chart is like looking at it through a magnifying glass: it makes the image bigger, but does not add detail. Note that the pixels are becoming obvious.

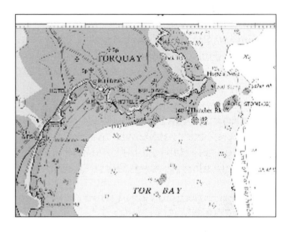

Zooming out on a raster chart is like stepping back for a wider view: the image is smaller, but nothing is removed from it.

you need just the same number of charts if you are using ARCS as if you are navigating on paper.

Vector charts

The important difference between raster and vector charts is that although a vector chart is usually based on several raster charts, its production process includes a significant extra stage, in which the raster image is electronically 'traced'.

This converts the 'photographic' raster image into a 'graphic' image, more like that used in computer design programmes. Features such as contours, which appear on a raster chart as strings of pixels, are converted back into lines, defined by some of the positions they pass through and the extent to which they are bent.

Point objects, such as buoys and chimneys, which appear on the paper chart as symbols and on the raster chart as clusters of pixels forming the shape of the relevant symbol, are stored, in the vector chart, as a cross-reference into a library of information. This database of information is an integral part of the electronic chart, but in some ways it's rather more like the entry you might find in an almanac or list of lights, because it contains details of the feature itself, rather than of the symbol that appears on the paper chart.

In the early days of chart plotters, the main reason manufacturers were prepared to go to all this trouble was that computer memory was relatively bulky and expensive, particularly in a small and specialist

market, so the companies that produced dedicated hardware plotters needed charts that used as little storage space as possible, and which could be converted back into images on the screen with as little computer power as possible.

Those considerations are less important now, but they still have a part to play because in order to make them rugged and reliable, yet still affordable, most hardware chart plotters still use memory cards or cartridges rather than CD ROMs, and most still have screens that are much smaller than that of a typical laptop computer.

The reason for the growing popularity of vector charts, however, is that they combine this limited demand for storage space with a degree of flexibility that has prompted some people to call them 'intelligent' charts. Some plotters, for instance, can be programmed to sound an alarm if you cross a pre-set contour line; others can be persuaded to do the same thing pre-emptively if you plan a route that passes through such shallow water; while others can create a graphic 'fish's eye' view of the underwater landscape, modelled from the contours.

Vector charts are available in many different forms, from several different suppliers, but the most popular are 'cartridges' containing a solid-state memory chip in a plastic housing about the size of a postage stamp, and containing about 16 or 32 megabytes of data. This is equivalent to only about 2.5–5% of a compact disc, but vector charts are so economical in their use of memory that a single cartridge is still sufficient to give good coastal coverage of several hundred miles of coastline with pilotage detail – often right down to the level of individual moorings – for every port and harbour.

Updates are usually achieved through a 'service exchange' system, in which a retailer will take an old chart cartridge in

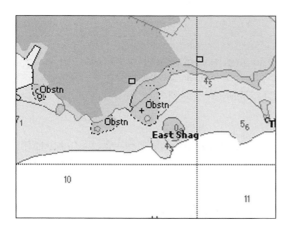

A vector chart looks different – and its appearance may change depending on the software used to view it.

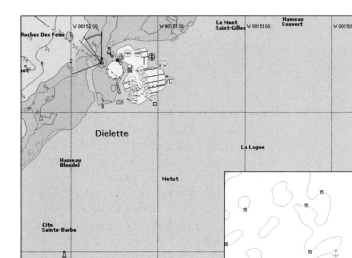

The plotter screen is like a window onto the chart, which can be scrolled or panned to reveal the areas you are interested in.

exchange for a new one, for about 25–33% of the price of a new cartridge.

▶▶ Despite their similarities, chart cartridges from different suppliers are physically and electronically incompatible: if possible, choose the manufacturer whose charts you prefer, and then find a plotter that accepts that type of cartridge.

Moving around a vector chart

Quite a few 'old school' navigators are put off hardware plotters by the small screen. 'I could never navigate on that', they say. 'It's like peering through a letterbox'.

Of course, they have a point. The Admiralty's compact 'Leisure' charts are nearly 70cm across the diagonal, equivalent to a 27-in screen, but even a 'big' plotter is unlikely to have a display much bigger than 10in. For most of us, a 7-in model is a more realistic option, giving a picture that's about as big as a Leisure

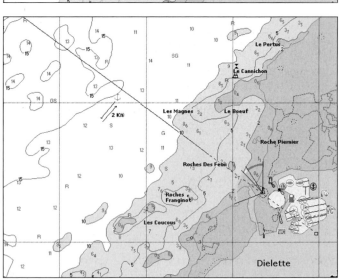

Most vector chart software has a 'declutter' facility to remove surplus information. Switching off the declutter restores the hidden detail – compare these two pictures (above).

folio chart that has been folded in half, and half, and half, and half again.

This 'letterbox' comparison, though, misses an important feature of plotters, which is that you don't *have* to navigate – at least, not in the sense of drawing lines, and plotting positions. Your job, as the intelligent part of the man-machine partnership,

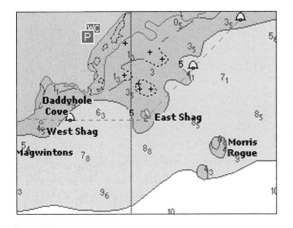

Zooming in on a vector chart is like changing to a more detailed chart: the image is bigger, and detail that was hidden on smaller scales is reinstated.

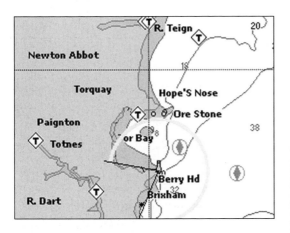

Zooming out on a vector chart is like changing to a smaller scale chart. There is almost no limit to the area that can be viewed at once: clutter is automatically removed, but symbols and labels remain legible.

is to make decisions, based on the information the plotter provides.

Making good use of an electronic plotter involves a basic familiarity with its controls, and in particular with those that allow you to move around the chart image, to look at different areas, or to look at larger or smaller areas. The **pan** and **scroll** controls appear to move the chart past the window of the display, and usually take the form of either a rocker pad or a cluster of four buttons, each marked with an arrow. The **zoom in** and **zoom out** controls are often marked with a magnifying glass, or with the symbols + and –. Their purpose is almost self-evident – but not quite.

▶▶ Between them, the pan, scroll, and zoom controls will more than make up for the small screen size, so long as you are not afraid to use them.

The magnifying glass symbol that is often used for the zoom controls is self-explanatory, but misleading, because on a vector chart – unlike a raster chart – zooming in does a lot more than just make the picture bigger; it also reveals more detail.

Of course, it can't add anything that isn't stored on the original cartridge; what happens is that the software built into the plotter will decide on an appropriate level of detail for the scale of the picture you are looking at, so it will remove detail as you zoom out, to make the picture clearer, but will reinstate it as you zoom in.

▶▶ If you want more information about a specific object, such as a lighthouse, most plotters will give it to you if you use the pan and scroll control to position the cursor over the object.

Decluttering is only available on vector charts. In effect, each type of information is stored in a different database: contour lines in one; spot soundings in another; major

On a vector chart, added information is often available by 'interrogating' the symbols representing navigational features.

lighthouses in another; buoys in another; and so on. The effect is rather as though a paper chart were built up using many different layers of tracing paper, each of which can be removed or replaced at will. Most software programs add and remove some layers automatically as you zoom in and out, in order to stop the screen becoming cluttered. Many, however, also allow you to choose 'more detail' or 'less detail', or to make your own selection of exactly what kind of information you want to see. It's

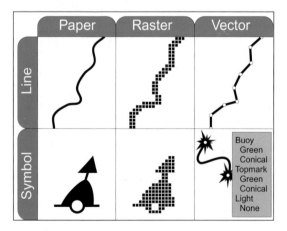

Fig 31 *The fundamental differences between raster, vector, and paper charts.*

important to appreciate, though, that the accuracy of information depends on the scale of the original chart, not on the zoom level you happen to have chosen, and to be aware that it is possible to inadvertently hide information which could turn out to be important.

There's one more control that is worth getting to grips with from the outset: the 'Find vessel' function. It may be a single button, a clever combination of keystrokes on the machine's control panel, or it may involve selecting from a menu. It may even be called something completely different! Whatever it's called, though, it is probably one of the most useful features of a chart plotter, because it will instantly change your view of the chart to put your own vessel at the centre of the screen.

Passage planning on a plotter

The fundamentals of passage planning don't change, whether it is being done on paper for traditional navigation, on paper for use with a GPS, or on a chart plotter.

You still have to devise a plan that:

- Achieves your objectives – whether that is 'going somewhere nice for lunch' or 'getting to the finish line'.

- Avoids hazards such as rocks, shallows, tide races, and prohibited areas.

- Allows for constraints such as sunrise and sunset, locks and swing bridges, tides and tidal streams.

Waypoints on a plotter

The principles of waypoint navigation don't change just because you're using a plotter rather than a GPS. The 'knobology' of which buttons to press or which menus to select from varies considerably from one plotter to another, but it is generally much easier than on a GPS, because it can be

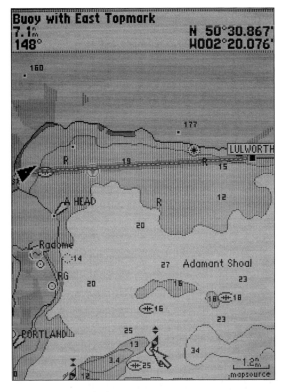

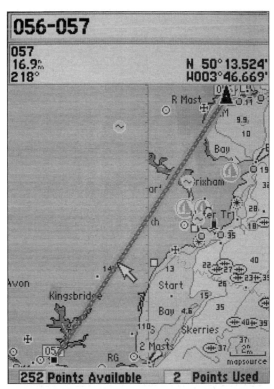

Above: A single-leg 'Go To' route, set up on a Garmin plotter. The first stage in setting up a more complex route (above right) is to tell the plotter where you are starting, and where you are going. The direct route (right) is obviously impractical, but extra waypoints can be inserted, to stretch the route around obstructions.

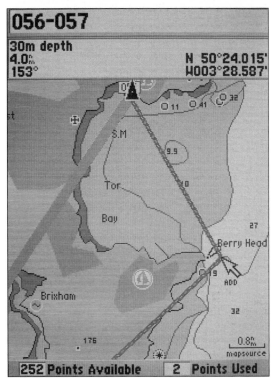

carried out graphically, by using the plotter's cursor to point to wherever you want the waypoint to be.

Suppose that we're leaving Weymouth, intending to go to Lulworth Cove, some seven miles along the coast to the east. On some hardware plotters, setting up this kind of simple, straight-line route involves no more than placing the plotter's cursor somewhere just outside the entrance to the cove, and pressing the 'Go To' button.

Only if you have to go to a precise position, such as a race mark, is it worth using the latitude and longitude facility.

Routes on a plotter

The control systems of most plotters are designed to make setting up more complicated routes as easy as possible. Unfortunately, different designers have very different ideas about how this can best be achieved, so, again, the knobology varies between different plotters.

In many cases, it's as simple as placing the cursor where you want to make the first turn, pressing <enter>, moving the cursor to the next turning point, and pressing <enter> again, and so on.

So long as you remember to keep an eye on where the route lies, rather than concentrating exclusively on the waypoints, there is nothing wrong with this A-to-B-to-C approach.

An alternative method of route planning uses a facility known as 'rubber banding'.

Suppose, for instance, that we're planning a passage from Torquay to Salcombe. We probably know where we're going from and to at a pretty early stage in the planning process, so it makes sense to put those two important waypoints in first, zooming in to look in detail at the area around Torquay, then zooming out to move the cursor and zooming in again to look at the entrance to Salcombe.

It's pretty obvious that a straight line route won't do in this case, because it passes right over a sizeable chunk of Devon, but the 'Insert Waypoint' facility allows us to add waypoints in the middle of the route, and move them so that the route stretches like a rubber band around various headlands and sandbanks on the way.

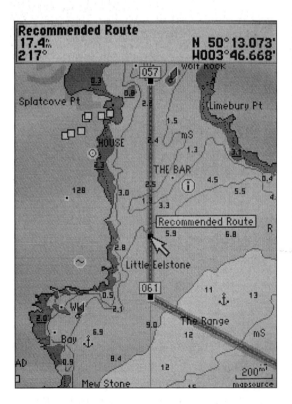

Zooming in gives a close-up and detailed view of tricky areas, and allows waypoints to be positioned accurately...

...while zooming out gives a clear view of the big picture.

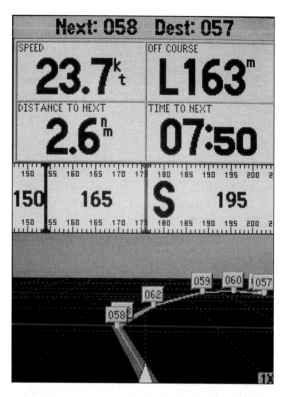

Next: 064	Dest: 057
SPEED	TO COURSE
0.0 k/t	**220** °/M
[bar graph] 8X	OFF COURSE **R105** m

056-057

Waypoint	Distance ◄	Course ►
064	0.2 n/m	152 M
058	4.2 n/m	195 M
063	4.6 n/m	201 M
062	7.6 n/m	216 M
059	16.7 n/m	255 M
060	20.6 n/m	302 M
061	23.0 n/m	
	23.6 n/m	218 M

Most plotters offer a route summary, including the distance and direction between each waypoint along the route.

In this case, the 'rolling road' display is just one of several pieces of information available on the helmsman's screen, and shows the whole route as though it were a winding road.

This technique involves a lot of zooming in and out – but that's one of the good things about it; at every stage you're combining a fairly broad overview of each leg with a more detailed look at each waypoint.

The other advantage of this technique is that it helps you to put waypoints where you need them, rather than where there happens to be a convenient mark on the chart.

Overlays

There are all sorts of pieces of information that could be superimposed onto a basic navigational chart. Some of these, such as

details of buoys and lighthouses, are already built into vector charts. Many vector charts also include information from which suitably-equipped plotters can calculate the height of tide at any given time, for various key places such as harbour entrances.

At the top of the list are tidal streams and weather information. These two are so fundamental to almost any passage that it seems odd that they are not virtually standard. At present, though, very few 'hardware' plotters are capable of presenting this kind of information, although it is fast becoming a feature of all but the most basic chart plotting software available for PCs.

Tidal streams

Tidal stream data can be regarded simply as an electronic tidal stream atlas. Information is stored in the PC in much the same way as a vector chart, with geographical locations on the chart linked to databases of the tidal stream at each location. Of course, the tidal streams are constantly changing, so the programme also needs the astronomical data required to work out which particular bit of tidal stream information applies to which particular time. It all adds up to a surprisingly complex package: perhaps this is why it is often sold as a separate 'module', available as an optional add-on to more basic chart plotting software.

Merely displaying tidal stream information is one thing, but to make it really

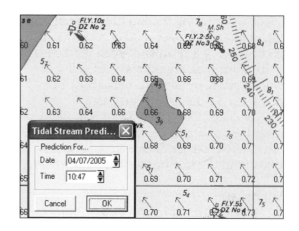

Tidal stream data is usually only available on PC-based systems, often as an expensive additional 'module'.

worthwhile, most programmes are able to assess the effect of the ever changing tidal stream on a planned route; they can calculate the course to steer from each waypoint to the next, display the predicted ground track and ETA, and in many cases can work out the best time to leave in order to make 'best' use of the tidal streams.

Bear in mind, though, that they are not

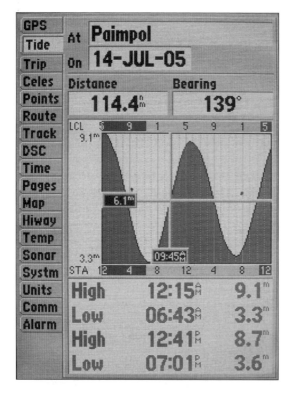

Many hardware plotters offer quick and accurate tidal height information.

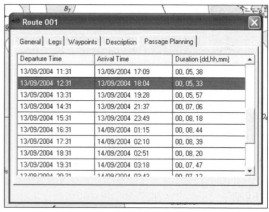

A PC plotter with a tidal stream module included can be expected to be able to calculate the optimum course to steer between waypoints, and possibly even advise you of the optimum time to set off.

capable of making the kind of judgements that a human skipper might: they may suggest rounding a headland when the tide is at its maximum, regardless of the effect of any overfalls, or advise a powerboat skipper to set off on an upwind passage when the wind and tide are against each other, regardless of the fact that he may be able to travel ten knots faster in a flatter sea if he waits until the tide has turned 'against' him.

Weather

Weather information, of course, cannot be sold on CDs and stored in the computer for months without becoming out of date, so a vital pre-requisite of any practical weather overlay system is some form of communication with the outside world. For coastal sailors, this need be no more than a mobile phone to provide a dial-up connection to the internet, where there are numerous websites that provide weather information in the form of 'GRIB' (GRIdded Binary data) files.

The 'grid' in question is a network of imaginary lines, dividing a part of the Earth's surface into square boxes, rather like the grid lines on an Ordnance Survey map. Once the first part of the GRIB file has defined its grid (and one or two other variables, such as time), the main part of the file is devoted to a coded description of the weather at each grid intersection in turn.

There are plenty of relatively simple programmes available that can display the information contained in a GRIB file, even

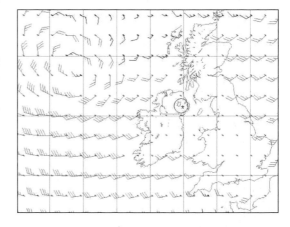

Gridded binary (GRIB) files contain weather information and forecasts and are available from various internet sources.

Course to steer by mental arithmetic or pocket calculator

Even if you're using a hardware plotter, or simple PC software that can't handle tidal streams, there's a simple and quick alternative to digging out the paper chart to calculate a course to steer. The basic rule is:

Multiply the tidal stream by 60 and divide by your boat speed

The answer is the number of degrees you should add or subtract to your intended track. Subtract the offset if the tidal stream is pushing you to starboard, and add it if the tidal stream is pushing you to port. Remember it as 'port plus, starboard subtract'.

For tidal streams that are over the bow or quarter, rather than directly abeam, use about half the tide speed, rather than its full value.

For course to steer over periods of longer than an hour, use the average tidal stream over the period, remembering that if it changes direction completely, one way should be treated as negative.

The result is theoretically less accurate than one based on the same calculation using traditional chartwork, but in practice, any errors introduced by the arithmetic are likely to be far smaller than those caused by inaccurate chartwork, inaccurate tidal stream data, or errors in the estimated speed.

showing how something such as wind strength and direction is likely to change over a period of time. Some of these programmes are even available as 'freeware', that can be downloaded at no charge straight from the internet.

Some of the more sophisticated chart plotting programmes, however, take this further; if the owner takes the trouble to supply the necessary information about how fast the boat will move on different points of sail and different wind strengths, the programmes will build the predicted speed into the passage plan, even using a process of trial and error to find the optimum route between waypoints.

This sounds tempting, and for would-be record-breakers and those at the sharp end of offshore racing fleets, it is bordering on essential, but cruising sailors and motor-boaters need to treat these programmes with a degree of caution. Remember that every extra feature and function breeds complexity. If you are discouraged by menus and dialogue boxes, you may well find that driving the computer is more complicated than making the same decisions by calculation and intuition.

7

PCs on board

For many owners, it's the versatility of a PC that leads them into electronic charting in the first place. Rather than running other programmes on a computer that has been acquired specifically as a navigation tool, they find themselves installing navigation software on a laptop that was originally intended for work.

Laptops

In principle, at least, a laptop needs no 'installation' at all: you simply carry it on board, and plug in the GPS. It's a good idea to have something to stop it from sliding off the chart table, but that can be as

Even a basic laptop computer can run most chart plotting software.

simple as a loop of thin string or a couple of strips of Velcro. Neater, safer, and more long-term installations may involve a custom-built wooden box on the chart table or nearby shelf.

Built-in PCs

The very low price of office PCs, particularly second-hand ones, lends a certain appeal to the idea of building one into a locker.

Unfortunately, that low price is only partly achieved by economies of scale. Production costs are also kept down by using quite large circuit boards, supported only at their edges. This is fine in the stable, stationary environment for which they were designed, but in a moving boat they are likely to flex, and will ultimately fatigue and break.

A supplementary problem is that powerful processors generate a significant amount of heat, which has to be disposed of.

Both problems can be solved by using a 'ruggedised' or 'marinised' PC, built using smaller circuit boards that are better supported, with shock-proof mountings for its heavier components. The whole case is likely to be more robust, with mounting lugs so that it can be bolted down, and it may well have been designed to operate on a 12v DC power supply.

▶▶ None of this comes cheap; expect to pay at least three times as much for a marine PC without a monitor or controls as for a complete desktop PC package deal.

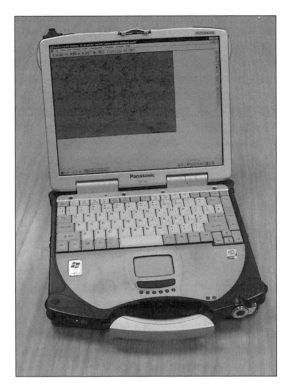

'Ruggedised' computers, like this Panasonic Toughbook, generally have smaller screens and are much more expensive than standard laptops, but are better suited to life afloat.

Power supplies

Although computers use 12v DC for some purposes, such as powering their monitors and the motors that drive their cooling fans and disc drives, they use much lower voltages for their processors and memory – typically in the order of 3–5v. To make sure that each component receives the right voltage at the right time, the computer includes its own automatic transformer and distribution system. In the case of office and industrial PCs, this is designed to accept normal AC mains power. Laptops, on the other hand, usually require between 15 and 24v DC, usually through a compact mains-powered transformer.

If your PC is designed to run on mains power, there are two options open to you. One is to invest in an inverter, to convert the boat's 12v DC supply into a reasonably close copy of the mains 240v AC output. An economical 'modified sine wave' inverter will do, but it needs to be able to sustain an output of at least 250 watts. The alternative is to have the PC's original 'power supply' replaced by one that is intended to operate on 12v DC. The latter is more expensive, but it's much safer and more efficient.

An inverter (this one cost £20) is the easiest way to power a PC from a boat's batteries, so long as you are prepared to accept the risks of using 240v power on board.

Laptop users could opt for a rather smaller inverter, with an output of about 150 watts. An alternative is to use a DC-DC converter – often sold as a 'car-laptop power adaptor'.

This is unquestionably the best and neatest solution, so long as you check that the output is enough to charge the battery as well as just keep the laptop running: it needs to be rated at least 3 amps (or 50 watts). It's a good idea, too, to cut the cigarette lighter plug off the end, and hardwire the converter into the boat's electrical system, with a suitable fuse.

Inverters

There are various ways of making AC (alternating current) electricity from the DC (direct current) electricity stored in the boat's batteries:

- Ferroresonant inverters are generally heavy and reliable, but not very efficient.
- Switch mode inverters are lighter, smaller, and more efficient.
- Hybrid inverters are an attempt to combine the best of both worlds. They do so pretty successfully, but cost more than either of the others.

The output, of course, is more important than how it is achieved. In domestic mains electricity, the voltage constantly changes, so if you plotted it on a graph it would appear as a smooth sine curve. Pure sine wave inverters, usually of the ferroresonant type, achieve almost exactly the same thing. Switch mode inverters, however, usually produce a 'modified sine-wave' output, in which the voltage rises and falls in a series of steps. Most computers can run on either type.

Displays and controls

Again, the laptop user has a relatively simple life, because so far as the displays and controls are concerned, a boat isn't much different from the cars and trains for which his computer was designed.

▶▶ A separate tracker ball is a good investment, even if you are using a laptop.

If you've invested in a marinised or industrial PC, however, you have considerably more flexibility in the screen and controls you can install with it. It's unlikely that you will want to consider a conventional CRT monitor, so the first choice is definitely a slim, flat-screen TFT that will run from the boat's 12v supply, and can be screwed to a bulkhead without taking up too much space.

It's almost impossible to operate any computer software without a keyboard, even if you only use it for naming waypoints and entering latitude and longitude. Fortunately, keyboards are so cheap that they can be regarded almost as consumable items – keep one on and one spare!

▶▶ Don't bother with touch screens; they aren't precise enough, and some of them don't work with wet hands!

A look to the future

At present, hardware plotters outnumber on-board PCs by something like two or three to one.

It's easy to see why: an integrated, custom-built plotter is bound to be easier to

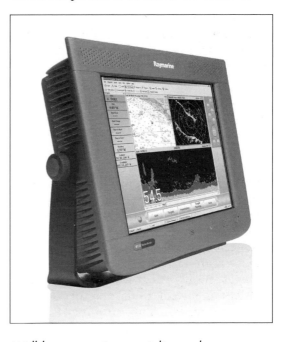

Well-known marine specialists such as Raymarine are now producing computer hardware that is designed for use afloat.

use and more reliable than the hotch-potch of hardware and software from different companies that makes up a PC-based system. And if a hardware plotter does go wrong, it's pretty obvious who to blame, so you won't be passed from one helpline to another, paying a pound a minute to be told that it's someone else's problem.

As time goes by, however, the distinction between hardware plotters and PCs is becoming more and more blurred. Hardware companies, such as Raymarine, are moving into PC software and producing multipurpose displays, while ruggedised PCs and laptops are becoming easier to find and less expensive.

It could well be that within a few years, the distinction will have all but disappeared, and we shall find ourselves buying a black or grey box that is designed to hide away under a bunk, linked to several screens and control panels dotted around the boat. One of those panels might control an autopilot, while another might switch the navigation lights on and off. One of the screens might carry the chart plotter and radar images, while another is showing the local TV station, or a feature film on DVD.

Intended mainly for commercial vessels, Simrad's CS56 combines a marine PC with a dedicated screen, and controls built into the arm-rest of the skipper's chair.

8

Echo sounders

Back in the Fifties, a typical small boat echo sounder weighed as much as a dinghy and outboard, and cost as much as a small car, so most yachtsmen relied on a lead weight on a length of line to measure the depth of water.

How they work

The principle of an echo sounder, however, is very simple, so when the first solid-state transistors came along to revolutionise consumer electronics, it wasn't long before the size and price of echo sounders plummeted, and they became standard equipment on all but the smallest and simplest of boats.

An echo sounder works by transmitting pulses of ultrasonic sound from a transducer mounted in the boat's hull. The pulses travel down to the seabed, and are reflected, to return to the boat as echoes. Sound, in sea water, travels at an almost constant speed of 1400m per second, so the time taken for each pulse to complete a down-and-back trip is directly proportional to the depth of water.

Analogue sounders

The simplest timing system, used in the first mass-market echo sounders of the late 1950s, and still used in a handful of models today, is known as the rotating neon or 'flasher' system, in which the heart of the display unit consists of a fast-spinning rotor with a miniature neon lamp or light-emitting diode at one end. Each time the rotor passes the upright position, the light flashes, and the transducer is triggered to

A typical echo sounder transducer for through-hull mounting. The black circular patch is the face of the transducer itself.

Flasher echo sounders are 'old' technology, but some people prefer them and a few companies still produce them in response to that demand.

transmit its pulse. When the returning echo hits the transducer, the energy is converted back into electricity, and amplified, to make the light flash again.

By this time, however, the rotor has moved on. How far it has moved depends on the time interval between transmission and reception, so the depth of water is indicated by the position of the second flash, and can be read directly from a scale marked on the face of the instrument, around the window that covers the rotor.

For operation in deep water, the rotor speed can be slowed down, increasing the range of time intervals that can be measured, and extending the interval between successive pulses.

With practice, the appearance of the second flash gives a good clue to the nature of the seabed: a bright but short flash indicates a hard seabed, while a softer seabed produces a softer, more drawn-out echo.

Fish-finders

An alternative to the flashing neon or flashing LED used exactly the same principle, except that instead of flashing a light against a scale, the returning echo triggered an electronic pen to make a mark on a paper roll, producing a graphical record of the changing depth.

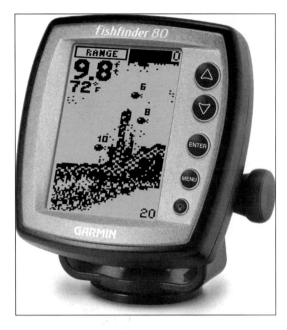

Fish-finders offer a graphic display at rock-bottom prices.

This pictorial record made it very easy to identify spurious echoes, as well as to spot changes in the real depth, but it was expensive, heavy, and used an awful lot of paper, so it was scarcely viable on small craft.

Then along came graphic displays and digital processing which, combined with

False echoes

Sometimes echoes can be misleading. Spurious flashes can sometimes be seen in shallow waters over a hard bottom, where the returning echo is bounced back from the surface of the sea to set off on its down and back trip all over again, to produce a 'reflection echo' or 'multipath echo', which shows up as a relatively weak echo at almost exactly twice the correct depth.

Misleading flashes can also appear in very deep water, in which the echo doesn't return until the rotor has completed one full revolution. The returning 'second trace' echo then produces a flash on the display, appearing to indicate much less than the true depth. If, for instance, the echo sounder is set to an operating range of 25m and the actual depth is 30m, the indicated depth will be 5m.

Air bubbles are good reflectors of sound, as are the air-filled swim-bladders of fish, so turbulence from passing ships or schools of fish can easily be mistaken for shallow water.

the basic echo sounder technology, produced the type of instrument that is now usually called a fish-finder. The most sophisticated fish-finders include all sorts of refinements designed to make them better at helping fishermen to find fish, but even the most basic models, selling for less than £100, are useful navigation instruments, whose pictorial display gives a very clear indication of which echo really represents the seabed, and how the depth of water is changing.

Digital echo sounders

The next step in development from the original flasher echo sounders were moving needle instruments, in which the depth of the strongest echo was displayed by a moving pointer against a dial. They were not destined to last long, however, before they were superseded by digital echo sounders, in which the depth was shown numerically, on liquid crystal displays.

These now account for the overwhelming majority of echo sounders, but are not

Digital echo sounders require surprisingly sophisticated technology, but usually give a clear and unambiguous reading.

quite as simple as they seem. The main snag is that the seabed may not be producing the strongest echo or the deepest, so the instrument needs to be able to distinguish between different types of echo. In general, modern echo sounders look for the strongest consistent echo; this prevents them from showing short-lived echoes from passing fish or debris, or from locking on to

Frequencies

Echo sounder transducers work in much the same way as the piezo electric crystals used to light gas cookers, using a man-made crystal of either lead zirconate or barium titanate. In the gas lighter, tapping the crystal (by pressing the button, or squeezing the trigger) produces a surge of electricity to create a spark. In an echo sounder transducer, the opposite happens: a pulse of electricity forces the crystal to vibrate. Then, when the echo returns, the faint vibrations of the echo returning to the crystal are enough to create a weak but detectable pulse of electricity.

The big difference between fish-finders and echo sounders is that navigators generally want to know the depth of water,

regardless of whether the transducer is pointing straight at it or not. This calls for a beam of sound energy that is not particularly well focussed, but is still powerful enough to reach the seabed. This is usually achieved by using crystals that are fairly small in diameter (typically 25mm or 38mm) and whose thickness is chosen to make them vibrate at 50,000 vibrations per second (50kHz).

Fish-finders, on the other hand, need to concentrate on 'looking' in a particular direction. This is best achieved by using the much higher frequencies of 192kHz or 200kHz. These higher frequencies are less good for penetrating great depths, but that problem can be overcome simply by making them more powerful.

weak but consistent second trace echoes.

At the same time, the built-in software tries to reduce the interval between pulses to a minimum, so as to gather as much information as possible. If you listen to the transducer in shallow water, you may be able to hear a regular pattern of faint clicks. In deep water, however, the pulses need to be further apart, so as to allow enough time for each returning echo to come back before the next pulse is transmitted. To make sure that this is happening, and as a defence against locking on to second trace echoes, the software will occasionally increase the interval between pulses. To anyone listening to the transducer, it will sound as though the echo sounder has 'missed a beat'. Don't worry; this is perfectly normal!

In spite of all this, digital echo sounders are easily confused by water turbulence, shoals of fish, or very shallow water. Readings from digital echo sounders should only be relied upon if the reading is consistent, and in keeping with what you would expect it to be from the charted depth and state of tide.

Forward-looking echo sounders

Forward-looking echo sounders are a relatively recent development. The principle is simple enough: if you direct an echo sounder's pulses forwards instead of downwards, it will measure horizontal distances instead of vertical ones. In practice, however, the technology is significantly more complex, so the equipment is considerably more expensive.

The main problem for the designer of a forward-looking sounder is that simply knowing that there is 'something within 50 metres' isn't good enough. To the navigator, there's a world of difference between something 50 metres away, and just below the surface, and something 35 metres ahead

but 35 metres deep, even though they are the same distance from the transducer.

To overcome this, the forward-looking sounder has to be able to identify the direction from which the echo is being received, as well as the distance, and to display the information in a graphical form. The graphic display need be no more complicated than that of a £100 fish-finder, but there are two distinct solutions to the direction problem. One is to focus the transmissions into a narrow beam, and to sweep the beam either up and down through the water ahead, or from side to side, like an underwater radar. The other is to transmit a wide beam, like an underwater floodlight, but use a directional sensor to listen for the returning echoes.

Both types are in production, and both have their virtues, but both suffer the overwhelming snag that sound travels relatively

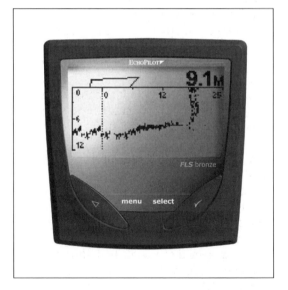

The display may look like that of a fish-finder, but the important feature of a forward-looking echo sounder is that it can give a graphic warning of underwater hazards ahead, rather than a historical record of what you have already sailed over. Unfortunately, the forward range is limited.

slowly. This means that if the instrument is to be able to look further forward than a few metres, there has to be a significant time interval between the pulses, while it listens for returning echoes. This, in turn, means that it takes a long time to build up a reasonably complete picture of what lies ahead.

Forward-looking sounders can be useful in very close-quarters pilotage, or for specialised jobs such as finding wrecks, but they can't be relied upon to avoid shipping containers, whales, or submarines in open water!

Installing an echo sounder

Most echo sounders consist of two main parts – a display unit and a transducer – with a fairly thin cable connecting the two, and a power cable to connect the display unit to the boat's 12v electrical system. Most of the clever business of generating and interpreting the pulses and echoes goes on inside the display unit, leaving the transducer with the relatively simple task of converting electrical pulses to sound and vice versa.

Some of the more sophisticated systems, however, use an 'active transducer', in which a supplementary box of tricks, close to the transducer, does all the calculation, and sends straightforward depth data to a multipurpose display. Others may use a black box called a 'hub' or 'central processor' to collect information from several sensors such as wind and speed transducers, and distribute it to a number of displays around the boat. Installing such systems is well within the scope of the average DIY boat-owner, but it's essential to read the manual before you start.

Installing a 'conventional' echo sounder in a typical GRP cruiser, however, is very straightforward.

The most important single task is to make sure the transducer is in the right place. It needs to be pointing downwards,

Echo sounder transducers can be mounted inside most GRP or metal hulls. Almost any transducer can be epoxied directly to the hull, but this one is designed specifically for in-hull mounting.

in an area of clear, undisturbed water flow, where it is unlikely to leave the water as the boat pitches or rolls. For most sailing boats, this is likely to be just in front of the keel, or slightly further aft and offset to one side.

On displacement motor boats, the optimum position is similar to that for sailing boats, but fast motor boats need to have their transducers mounted much further aft, to keep them in the water and well away from the turbulence where the bottom panels meet the water surface. On an inboard motor cruiser, this may mean at the aft end of the engine compartment or forward end of the space under the cockpit. Boats with outboard motors or outdrives can go even further, and have their transducers mounted close to the transom, or even on a bracket screwed to the outside of the transom. This latter option is particularly good for boats such as RIBs and ski-boats which are likely to be hauled out onto trailers, and can be worth considering for trailer-sailers as well.

▶▶ Make sure there are no skin fittings such as toilet inlets or outlets or engine cooling water inlets directly ahead of the transducer.

Transducers are usually supplied complete with skin fittings to allow them to pass through the hull of the boat, so that their transmitting face is in direct contact with the water. Some models even have the transducer and skin fitting combined in a single unit. This, however, is unnecessary for a GRP or metal hull. Although there may be some slight loss of deep water performance by mounting the transducer inside the boat, it is a price worth paying: the transducer is less likely to be damaged, and it means one less hole in the hull.

▶▶ Do not try to cut or splice an echo sounder cable. Leave any excess cable coiled up and tucked out of sight.

Internal mounting

First, make sure that the area in which you intend to mount the transducer is not hollow, nor of sandwich construction: the transducer must be mounted so that there is solid GRP between it and the sea. If necessary, you can cut away the inner skin and sandwich core, and seal the cut edges with epoxy resin, to leave the inner surface of the outer skin visible. This is rarely necessary, though: few boats use sandwich construction throughout, particularly along the centreline or around the keel.

The classic method of mounting an internal transducer then involves mounting a plastic tube, such as a short length of rainwater pipe so that it stands up vertically from the inside of the hull, using a fillet of epoxy resin to bond it to the hull and form an oil-proof joint. The transducer is then supported loosely inside the tube, just clear of the hull, and the intervening space filled with oil.

▶▶ Any oil will do! It doesn't have to be castor oil, but it is best to avoid oils with high concentrations of additives such as gear oil. Cooking oils are ideal.

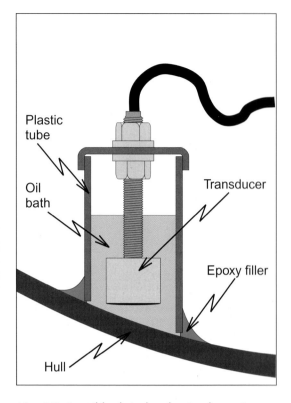

Fig 32 *An oil bath is the classic alternative to epoxy mounting.*

A simpler and more reliable alternative is to stick the transducer directly onto the inside of the hull using a slow-curing epoxy resin. Before doing so, however, it is best to check that the area is suitable by flooding the area with water (use Plasticine or something similar to build a miniature coffer dam around it, if you like), and stand the transducer in it. Connect everything up, and make sure it works. Assuming it does, dry the area thoroughly, and stick the transducer down.

Here, too, Plasticine or chewing gum is useful, because you need to achieve a perfectly rigid, air-free joint, and the best way to do that is by using a slow-curing liquid epoxy, rather than a paste. Use a thin strip of Plasticine to keep a pool of epoxy in place while you mount the transducer and allow the adhesive to harden.

▶▶ Don't be tempted to use any kind of flexible adhesive such as silicon sealant: it will absorb the sound energy from the transducer instead of transmitting it.

External mounting

An internal mounting can't be used in a wooden boat: the only option is to drill a hole in the bottom to take the transducer and its skin fitting. Sizes vary, but most are about two inches in diameter.

If the bottom panel slopes significantly at your chosen spot, it may also be necessary to make a 'fairing piece' to create a flat, horizontal surface big enough to take the flange of the skin fitting on the outside of the hull, with a matching fairing inside to provide a seat for the big nut that holds the skin fitting in place. It's important that the inner and outer surfaces are parallel to each other, and that the hole through them is big enough not to crush the transducer even if the wood swells when it gets wet.

Having drilled the hole through the hull and fairing pieces, the skin fitting is then pushed through from the outside, and its securing nut screwed onto it inside the hull to hold it in place. A generous bead of silicon sealant inside and out before it is tightened down ensures that the whole thing is watertight – and you can always back it up with a mound of epoxy or GRP around the securing nut if you want to. It's a two person job, particularly if the transducer and its cable are an integral part of the skin fitting, but on a new hull it's more nerve-wracking than difficult.

If you're replacing an existing log which used a significantly bigger skin fitting than your new one, you'll either need to bung up the old skin fitting with a wooden plug,

epoxied into place, or else have the old hole professionally repaired before cutting a new hole.

If the old skin fitting was smaller than the new one, the easiest way to enlarge the hole is to drive a wooden wedge or bung into the hole from outside, and then cut it off a few millimetres proud of the hull. The wedge will then hold the pilot drill and mandrel of a conventional hole saw.

▶▶ Do not tap the transducer through with a hammer, scratch it, or cover it with any more than a single thin coat of antifouling.

Calibrating an echo sounder

Although the instruction manuals of many echo sounders and fish-finders refer to 'calibration' there is really nothing the user can do to calibrate an echo sounder to allow for the changing temperature and salinity of sea water. A few models allow you to select 'salt' or 'fresh', but that is as far as it goes.

You can, however, choose which units the instrument uses to display depth, and whether it indicates depth from the surface, from the keel, or from the transducer.

As they leave their factories, all echo sounders are set up to display depth below the transducer, but they are all supplied with instructions explaining how to enter an 'offset' to increase or decrease the indicated depth to account for the depth of the keel or the distance between the transducer and the waterline. It's up to you which you prefer: depth below the keel errs on the side of pessimism, but depth below the surface is much more useful.

9

Logs

The term 'knot' as a measure of speed comes from the days when speed was measured by dropping a piece of wood overboard, attached to a long piece of string. The string had knots in it, at regular intervals, so the number of knots that were dragged overboard in a given time, as the ship sailed away from the piece of wood, gave an indication of speed.

This 'chip log' has long since given way to more sophisticated devices, including the mechanical Walker log and, more recently, to a variety of electronic logs, but the measurement of speed and distance is such a fundamental part of traditional navigation that the log – like the echo sounder – is widely regarded as a traditional instrument rather than an electronic one!

How it works

There are many ways of measuring the flow of water past a boat's hull, but by far the most common is the paddlewheel or impeller log.

As the name suggests, the key feature of this type of log is a paddlewheel. It is typically about 3cm in diameter, and is fitted at the end of a cylindrical probe which passes through a skin fitting in the boat's hull so that the paddlewheel can be turned by the passing water.

A magnet is built into one of the paddlewheel blades, while the probe includes a device known as a Hall-effect sensor. As the paddlewheel rotates, the sensor acts as a kind of electronic switch, producing a pulse of electricity every time the magnet

A log transducer, showing the paddlewheel. The screw cap and pin at the other end allow the whole transducer to be withdrawn from its housing for cleaning.

passes it. These pulses are counted by the display unit, which calculates the speed of the boat and the distance it has travelled.

Other kinds of log
Pitot
Pitot logs are simple, cheap, and are occasionally fitted to small powerboats. They work by measuring the pressure exerted by the water on the forward face of a tubular sensor. Their simplicity makes them reasonably reliable, but they are incapable of

reading speeds below about 10 knots, and are seldom very accurate. Nor do they include a distance-measuring facility.

Electromagnetic logs

Electromagnetic logs are based on the principle that electricity is created if you move a magnetic field past an electrical conductor. Sea water is a good conductor of electricity, so if it flows past a magnet, an electric current will be generated within it. The faster the water flows, the greater the current will be.

These sophisticated devices are very accurate and reliable, but unfortunately they are bulky, expensive, and power hungry as well, so they tend to be used only in commercial vessels and the very largest of recreational craft.

Sonic logs

Several kinds of log use sound waves. One type has two transducers mounted a little way apart, each producing a sequence of high frequency sound pulses ('clicks'), which is detected by the other. When the boat is stationary, the clicks travel at the same speed in both directions. As the boat starts moving, however, the time taken by the aft-going click to complete its journey reduces, while the forward-going click takes longer. By comparing the two, the log can calculate how fast the boat is moving.

Another version uses the Doppler effect, by transmitting high frequency clicks, and listening for the echoes received as they bounce back from particles of dirt or plankton in the water. When the boat is moving, particles approaching the transducer produce echoes at a higher frequency than those moving away from it. By comparing the two frequencies against the frequency it transmitted, the log can work out the boat speed.

Yet another version uses a sophisticated development of echo sounder technology. Using two piezo electric crystals mounted

in a single transducer, but operating at very much higher frequencies than a normal echo sounder, the ultrasonic log analyses the echoes received from plankton or scraps of debris about 15cm from the transducer. The two crystals transmit simultaneously, but because they are a few centimetres apart, the echoes they receive back from plankton or scraps of floating debris are slightly different. A microprocessor, built into the transducer, compares the echo patterns, to find out how quickly the particles are passing the boat.

Installing a log

Like an echo sounder, a typical log consists of a display and a transducer, connected by a length of cable which is usually permanently attached to the transducer before it leaves the factory. The big difference between a log and a sounder, so far as installation is concerned, is that a log impeller has to be outside the boat in order to work, regardless of the type of hull. The ultrasonic log is an exception; it can be mounted inside a metal or solid GRP hull.

As with an echo sounder, the first step in the installation is to decide where the sensor is to be located. The same general rules apply: it needs to be constantly immersed, clear of bubbles or turbulence, and certainly well away from a propeller. It doesn't necessarily have to point downwards, like an echo sounder transducer, but it does have to be easily accessible from inside the boat.

Drilling the hole is more nerve-wracking than difficult, and once you've done it, installing the skin fitting is a matter of applying a generous bead of silicon sealant around the edge of the hole, pushing the skin fitting through from outside, and tightening its securing nut inside. Be careful, when doing so, because many logs have skin fittings which have to be lined up with the boat's fore-and-aft line: check the installation instructions to be sure.

Finally, insert the log sensor or the blanking plug which is supplied to take its place when the transducer has to be removed.

Cleaning an impeller

The biggest single problem with paddle-wheel logs is that their impellers are easily slowed down by fouling or by debris, so at some stage you are bound to find yourself having to retract the impeller in order to clean it. Some owners delay the moment by retracting the impeller whenever the boat is not in use, but it still means the impeller has to be withdrawn on a fairly regular basis.

It can be done while the boat is afloat, but beware that as soon as the log probe is withdrawn from its skin fitting, you will have created an open hole in the bottom of the boat, so some flooding is inevitable. If you are quick and well prepared, however, it need not be very much. The secret is to have a bundle of rag or a towel close at hand, along with the blanking plug. Loosen the transducer, which may be secured with a 'bayonet' fitting or a pin or split ring, and gently pull it out of the skin fitting, while keeping your bundle of rag ready in the other hand.

As soon as the probe clears the top of the skin fitting, staunch the flow of water with the rag, while you pick up the plug and get it lined up with the hole. Finally, whip the cloth away and slide the plug into place.

Some manufacturers offer 'self sealing' skin fittings, incorporating a flap valve. This reduces the influx of water, but must not be relied upon to stop it altogether.

Replacing the sensor is exactly the same procedure but in reverse.

Don't try removing the log sensor when you're alone on the boat.

Calibrating a log

No hull-mounted log can be expected to be 100% accurate.

The boat may drag some water along with it, making the water flow past its transducer slightly less than the boat's speed through the water, or the impeller itself may not be spinning freely. Conversely, the water flow may be accelerated as it passes the keel or is sucked into the propellers, to make the log over-read.

The job of measuring and correcting log error is known as calibration, and involves measuring the time the boat takes to cover a known distance, and using this to calculate the true speed which can be compared with the speed shown by the log.

Any accurately-measured distance can be used, but the best ones are the 'measured distances' which have been set up especially for the purpose at many major ports and harbours. The start and end of the measured distance are usually marked by transit posts, with the distance and course to steer marked on the chart.

There's no reason, though, why you shouldn't use any distance that you can measure accurately on the chart, or even

A dedicated log display. Although it is showing speed at the moment, a press of a button switches it to showing distance travelled, or vice versa.

use the speed shown by a GPS set.

Choose a reasonably calm day, ideally at a time and place where the tidal stream is weak. Under power, settle the boat onto the required course well before you reach the beginning of the measured distance, in order to let the speed settle, and then hold that course and speed until you reach the end. Record the time at which you cross the start line and finish line, and keep a note of the actual log reading during the run. Then repeat the process, at the same log speed, in the opposite direction.

For each run, your average speed can be found by dividing the distance covered by the time taken. This, however, is your speed over the ground. To find your speed through the water, you need to add the two speeds together and divide by two to find the average. A more accurate result can be obtained by making four or six runs, but this can be a time consuming process, especially as log errors are seldom consistent across the whole speed range, so the calibration runs really need to be carried out at several different speeds, and repeated again once the log has been adjusted.

▶▶ Don't try to shorten the arithmetic by adding the times together and dividing the distance by that: you will get a different (and wrong) answer!

Compare your averaged speed with the speed shown by the log to find the log error, and consult the equipment instructions to find out how to correct it. A single pair of calibration runs is better than nothing, but ideally you should carry out at least four, at each of several representative speeds.

The calculation looks like this:

Measured distance	1852m (1.00 nautical mile)
Time (first run)	8min 38sec = 518sec = 0.1439 hours
Speed (over ground)	6.95 knots
Log speed	6.7 knots
Time (south-bound run)	10min 17sec =6317sec =0.1714 hours
Speed (over ground)	= 5.83 knots
Log speed	6.8 knots
Average speed over ground	6.39 knots
Average log speed	6.75 knots
Discrepancy	0.36 knots
Log over-reads by	5.6%

10

Electronic compasses

For centuries, compasses based on magne-tised rocks, rings, or needles have been some of our most important navigational tools. Now, though, they're up against a little gadget called a fluxgate.

A fluxgate compass has several advan-tages, but the one that's probably done most for its popularity is the ability to com-municate with other equipment such as autopilots and radars. A follow-on from this is that a fluxgate heading sensor can be fitted almost anywhere on the boat – so you can choose a spot where it is less prone to errors than in the magnetic chaos around the helm position.

How a fluxgate works

A fluxgate depends on the intimate rela-tionship between electricity and magnetism:

- When an electric current flows through a coil of wire, the coil becomes a magnet.

- When a magnet moves through a coil of wire, it generates electricity.

A transformer, for instance, consists of a coil of wire (the primary) around a metal core. When an alternating current (AC) flows through the primary, it makes the core into a magnet, whose north and south poles change ends every time the current reverses. Another coil, wrapped around the whole assembly, is called the secondary. So far as the secondary is concerned, the ever-changing magnetic field set up by the primary is just like a moving magnet, so it generates an electric current.

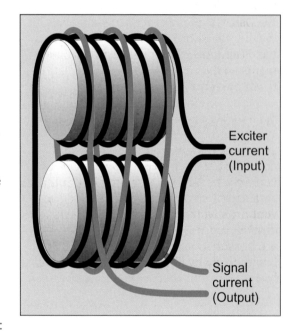

Exciter current (Input)

Signal current (Output)

Fig 33 *A single fluxgate element: a fluxgate compass usually has three (or more) elements arranged in a circular or star-shaped pattern.*

Structurally, a fluxgate is like a miniature transformer, except that it has two primary coils instead of one. They're made from the same continuous wire, but are wound in opposite directions. In a magnetically 'clean' environment, or when the cores are pointing east-west, the result is that the magnetic fields of the two primaries cancel each other out.

When the fluxgate is pointing north-south, however, the Earth's magnetic field upsets the balance, producing a current in the secondary winding.

A fluxgate compass is made up of several fluxgates arranged in a circle. By comparing the current generated in their secondary windings, it's possible to work out where north is, relative to the circle of fluxgates.

One big drawback of fluxgates is that they are notoriously susceptible to tilt, because tilting has much the same effect on the balance of magnetic fields inside as turning! To overcome this, most fluxgates have fluid mountings and gimbal arrangements that are at least as sophisticated as their 'swinging card' competitors.

Installation

To the user, all the inner workings of the compass and its gimbal system will almost certainly be hidden. Some models, intended as straightforward replacements for conventional steering compasses, do have a display, but most fluxgate heading sensors are housed in anonymous black or grey boxes, typically about the size of a tennis ball.

By far the most important factor to keep in mind when installing a fluxgate compass is that although it is electronic, it still works by detecting magnetic fields, so there is no point putting it right next to a substantial lump of metal such as an engine, a keel, or an anchor, or to anything (such as a loudspeaker) that contains a magnet or might create a magnetic field.

A secondary consideration is that the internal gimbal arrangements work best if they are not being bounced around too much. Of course, you can't expect a boat to stay perfectly still, but you can dramatically reduce the effects of pitch and roll by mounting the fluxgate unit somewhere near the boat's centre of gravity.

▶▶ For metal hulls, in particular, the first rule over-rides the second; a fluxgate compass will still work if it's mounted up a mast!

Having settled on the location, the actual installation is a simple matter of screwing

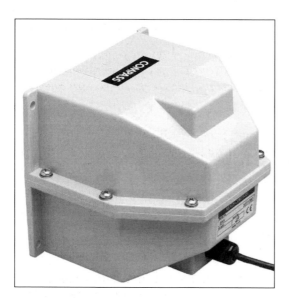

The fluxgate heading sensor is usually hidden away in a locker.

The output from a fluxgate can be used to drive a display like this, or it can be fed into other equipment, such as an autopilot or north-up radar.

the unit to a convenient bulkhead, making sure that its centreline (marked on the casing) is parallel to the centreline of the boat and that it is upright.

Electrical connections are equally straightforward, especially if the electronic compass is part of a package, such as an autopilot. In that case, all the connections will probably have been made for you, and all you have to do is to plug each plug into its matching socket! If you are trying to connect a compass from one company to a radar or autopilot from another, the important thing to remember is that you may not be dealing with NMEA 0183. Heading data can be presented in several different formats (codes) and it is important to make sure that the output from the compass is in a form that the other equipment can understand.

Self-correction

Another big plus point of most electronic compasses is their automatic correction facility. So far as the user is concerned, this usually involves little more than motoring round in a couple of slow circles.

▶▶ Read the manual!

What's going on in the compass's software, however, is pure mathematical magic. It's based on the fact that the current generated in a fluxgate should be related to the direction in which it is pointing, so on a polar diagram, it should be represented by a perfectly circular plot.

During calibration, an electronic compass monitors the changing output of its fluxgates, taking a lot of sample readings. Each sample spans a very short time interval, but together they supply enough information for the software to build up a virtual polar diagram of what is actually happening – which usually works out as a wobbly ellipse.

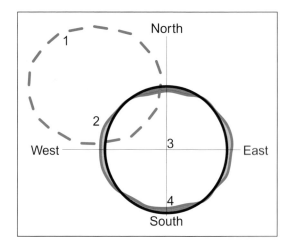

Fig 34 *Fluxgate automatic calibration:*
1 *The fluxgate software samples the output from the fluxgates.*
2 *It builds up a complete polar diagram from the samples.*
3 *It finds the centre of the polar diagram.*
4 *It compares the actual polar diagram with the perfect circle.*

It then carries out a two-stage mathematical process, first finding the circle which comes closest to matching it, and then working out the difference between the ellipse and the circle on each heading. These differences are then stored, and subsequently applied as corrections to remove the effect of deviation.

Calibration tips

- Calibration is easy, so do it often!
- Calibrate in calm water, well clear of large metal structures.
- The slower you circle, the better the results.
- Calibration cannot cope with magnetic fields stronger than that of the Earth, so mount the fluxgate sensor well clear of loudspeakers, DC wiring, and large metal objects.

11

Radar – how it works

Of all the electronic equipment available to navigators, radar is – to my mind, at least – the king. Surprisingly, perhaps, it's also one of the oldest: the German scientist Christian Hülsmeyer took out British and German patents on the basic principle of radar as early as 1904.

First principles

Measuring range

Whilst the technology involved in even the most basic of small craft radars is quite sophisticated, the principle by which a radar measures range is simple. It's very similar to that of an echo sounder: the radar transmits short pulses of energy, and then 'listens' for the returning echoes.

One major difference between a radar and an echo sounder is that the radar uses super high frequency radio waves, sometimes called microwaves, instead of sound. Radio waves travel at the speed of light

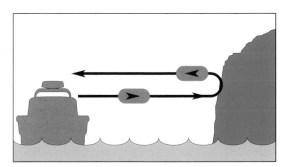

Fig 35 Radar finds the range of an object by measuring the time interval between when a pulse of microwave energy is transmitted, and when it returns as an echo.

(about 162,000 nautical miles per second), compared with the sluggish 1400 metres per second achieved by sound in sea water, so everything happens very much faster.

Typically, a small craft radar pulse lasts less than a millionth of a second, and the radar may transmit a thousand of them or more every second.

Suppose, for instance, that the radar transmits a pulse, and receives an echo 100 microseconds later. The total time taken for the pulse to make its out and back trip is 0.0001 seconds, so it has travelled 16.2 miles, which means that the object that reflected it must be 8.1 miles away.

Measuring bearing

Another obvious difference between a radar and an echo sounder is that whilst an echo sounder is used only to measure depth – and must therefore point its beam of sound energy straight downwards – a radar measures horizontal distances in any direction. Back in the 1930s, some of the very earliest shore-based radars achieved this by flooding a wide area with radio energy, and then using sensitive radio direction finders to measure the bearing of the returning echoes. This, however, is a very wasteful approach. Every modern marine radar uses a directional aerial to focus its microwave transmissions into a narrow beam that can be swept around the horizon.

The same aerial is used to catch the returning echoes. In other words, an echo will only be received if the aerial is pointing

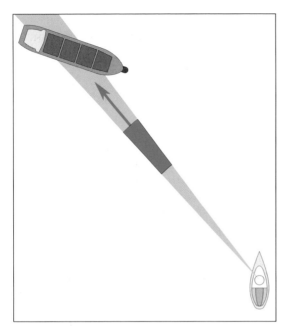

Fig 36 *The antenna (also known as the scanner or aerial) focusses the microwave pulses into a tight beam. The direction of an object is indicated by the direction in which the antenna is pointing when the echo is received.*

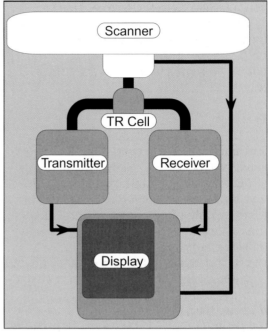

Fig 37 *The main parts of a radar set. In practice, everything except the display is combined into a single 'scanner unit' or 'radome'.*

at a solid object[3], so the direction the aerial is pointing in when it receives an echo is an indication of the bearing of the object that produced the echo.

Main components

In order to achieve all this, and to present the range and bearing information in a way that is comprehensible to a human operator, a radar set is made up of a number of major components. They are usually divided between two separate units – commonly called the **scanner** and the **display** – linked by a fairly substantial multi-core cable. Exactly which components are in which unit, however, varies to some extent depending on the make and model of radar.

[3]This isn't strictly true, but it's close enough for an explanation of general principles.

Transmitter

The heart of the transmitter is a special kind of electronic valve, known as a magnetron. Like the magnetron in a microwave cooker, its job is to generate the microwaves.

As with any radio transmitter, the frequency and wavelength of the radio waves it produces is an important factor in the performance of the radar. In most small craft radars, the frequency is approximately 9.4GHz (9,400,000,000 cycles per second), equivalent to a wavelength of about 3cm. For this reason, they are often described as '3cm radars', or 'X-band'. Some of the bigger, more powerful sets used by commercial ships, however, operate at about 3GHz, with a wavelength of about 10cm. You don't have to be a genius to guess that they are often known as '10cm radars', though you may also hear the term 'S-band'.

Three other characteristics of the transmitter play an important part in the performance of the radar as a whole: the *power*, *pulse repetition frequency* and *pulse length*.

Power
The effect of power might seem obvious: if you transmit more power, then the echoes produced by distant objects will be stronger, so they will be easier to detect. You might, therefore, expect a 4kW radar to be capable of detecting smaller objects than a 2kW radar, or of detecting large objects at a greater range. Up to a point, you would be right. It's important to appreciate, though, that radar waves – like light waves – travel in more or less straight lines, so they don't bend to follow the curvature of the Earth. This means that the maximum range at which you can expect a radar to detect distant objects is limited by the radar horizon, just as your ability to see distant objects is limited by the visual horizon.

Pulse repetition frequency (PRF)
This refers to the number of pulses transmitted in one second. In small craft radars, it varies from about 2000 pulses per second to less than one thousand, so the interval between pulses (the **pulse repetition interval**, or PRI) typically ranges from about 500 microseconds to about 1500 microseconds. The reason for such 'long' intervals between pulses is to make sure that all the echoes that could possibly have been produced from one pulse will have had time to get back to the antenna before the next pulse is transmitted.

Pulse length
The pulse length also varies. Typically, it's about one tenth of a microsecond when the radar is operating in short range mode, and up to about one microsecond when in long

range mode. A simple analogy is to compare a golf ball and a ping-pong ball. You can't throw a ping-pong ball very far, because it is so light that it doesn't have much energy. A golf ball, on the other hand, can be thrown much further because it is heavy, so when you throw it at the same speed as the ping-pong ball, you give it more energy. Both balls expend energy in overcoming the resistance of the air, but the golf ball has more energy to begin with, so it doesn't slow down as quickly, and travels further. Like most simple analogies, this isn't technically perfect, but it makes the point that a long pulse, like a golf ball, can travel further because it has been given more energy. A short pulse, like the ping-pong ball, travels less far because it has less energy.

This, of course, begs the question 'why bother with short pulses?' The answer is that short pulses enable the radar to discriminate between targets that are close together – a property known as **range discrimination**.

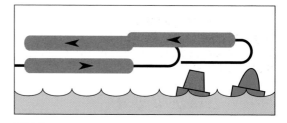
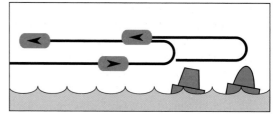

Fig 38 *Long pulses give good range, but poor discrimination. Short pulses give better discrimination, but poor range. Most radars automatically select an appropriate pulse length for the range scale in use.*

Imagine, for a moment, that it is possible to see the radar pulse emerging from the antenna like a sausage coming out of a butcher's sausage machine. As the transmitter starts transmitting, the pulse begins to emerge, with its leading edge travelling outwards at 162,000 miles per second. One microsecond later, the transmitter stops transmitting, so the trailing edge of the pulse leaves the antenna. It, too, travels outward at 162,000 miles per second, but it's already 300m behind the leading edge and can never catch up.

Now suppose the pulse comes across two buoys. They are on the same bearing from the radar but one is 100m further away than the other. The leading edge of the pulse hits the first one, and some of its energy is reflected back towards the radar. A fraction of a microsecond later, the leading edge reaches the second buoy, and is again reflected back towards the radar. On its way, it passes the first buoy, which is still receiving – and reflecting – energy from the same pulse. The two echoes merge, so on the radar screen the two buoys will appear as a single, large object.

A long pulse can't discriminate between two objects that are less than about 150m apart: a short pulse, by contrast, may be only 20m long, so it can separate objects that are only about 10m apart.

Antenna

Like any radio, a radar needs an antenna to get the radio waves from its transmitter into the outside world, and to capture the returning echoes. Unlike the more familiar antennas used on car radios or marine VHF sets, however, a radar antenna is not expected to be equally effective in all directions: we want it to focus the microwave energy into a beam, and to sweep the beam around the horizon like the rotating beam of a lighthouse.

There are several ways of achieving this.

One of the simplest is to use a **parabolic reflector**, rather like the reflector of a car's headlamp. Another is to make use of a device known as a **slotted waveguide**. A waveguide is essentially a metal tube through which microwaves flow like water through a hose pipe. Cutting slots in the waveguide allows the microwave energy to escape, just as the holes in a lawn sprinkler allow the water to escape. The third, and increasingly common alternative, is to use a **patch array** made up of a number of little copper pads, each no bigger than a 5p piece. Each pad acts as a small antenna, but their cumulative effect is very much like the array of slots in a slotted waveguide.

Beamwidth

Whichever type of antenna is used, the inescapable fact of life is that if you want a narrow beam, you need a big antenna. The very smallest radars, for instance, have antennas about 12in (30cm) across, and produce a fan-shaped beam about 7° wide. The biggest radars aimed at small craft have scanners about 4ft (1.2m) across, and a beamwidth of 2°, while the 10–12ft scanners that are often fitted to commercial shipping can achieve beamwidths of less than one degree.

A small beamwidth is a good thing because it intensifies the power of the radar, just as the lenses of a lighthouse create an intense beam that is visible for many miles from a lamp that in some cases is no more powerful than an ordinary domestic light bulb.

Even more importantly, a radar with a narrow beamwidth will have very much better **bearing discrimination** than one with a wider beamwidth. Just as range discrimination refers to the radar's ability to separate two targets that are on the same bearing but at slightly different ranges, bearing discrimination refers to its ability to separate objects that are at the same

Fig 39 *Radar cannot 'see' the gap between two targets unless the gap is big enough for the beam to pass straight through.*

to the left of it, and would go on doing so until it was pointing 2° to the right of the buoy. On the radar screen, the buoy would appear to be 4° across. As the scanner sweeps round further, however, the beam would pass straight through the gap between the two buoys, so no echo would be received. A moment later, of course, the beam would illuminate the other buoy, and apparently enlarge that to 4° as well. The point is, however, that there was a point between the two buoys at which neither of them was illuminated, so no echo was received. In other words, the radar could see the gap.

If your radar had a beamwidth of 7°, that would not be the case. At no stage would the beam be able to pass through the 6° gap without being reflected from one buoy or the other, so on the screen, both buoys would be enlarged so that their edges appear to fuse together.

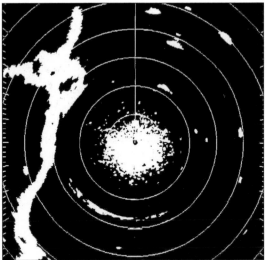

Another effect of beamwidth is shown in this picture of a radar screen, taken just off Dover. The blobs on the right-hand side are ships, expanded by the effect of beamwidth. Just below centre and to the left, the curving 'smear' is the effect of side lobe echoes, returned from a ship that is broadside-on.

range but on slightly different bearings.

Imagine a radar beam as though it were a torch beam, shining towards two buoys that are half a mile away but 100m apart. If you took a bearing of them, you would find that they were 6° apart. If your radar has a beamwidth of 4° it would start illuminating one buoy when the scanner is pointing 2°

The effect of a big beamwidth can be compared with a picture drawn using a thick felt-tip pen: small objects may be enlarged, but they tend to merge together so the overall result is a loss of definition.

Vertical beamwidth

Although we are most often concerned with the two-dimensional world represented by the surface of the water, the chart, or a radar screen, it's worth remembering that the real world is three-dimensional, and that radar beams have height, as well as width!

The vertical beamwidth of a radar has a much less noticeable effect on a radar's performance than its horizontal beamwidth, and is usually very much bigger – usually about 25° or 30°. Having such a big vertical beamwidth is certainly somewhat wasteful of power, but it's an important feature of a practical marine radar, for the simple reason that boats seldom stay level for very long. If the vertical beamwidth were only 6°, and the boat rolled more than 3°, then the radar beam on one side would be pointing down to the sea, while on the other side it would be pointing up in the air. A large vertical beamwidth ensures that for angles of heel of up to about 15°, at least some of the radar beam will always be directed towards the horizon.

Side lobes

All this discussion of antenna characteristics so far has made the unwritten assumption that the radar beam has perfectly defined edges, and that all the radar's transmitted power is contained within the beam. Sadly, real radars are not that perfect, and in real life the beam has fuzzy edges. Most radar antennas also produce a number of weaker beams called side lobes alongside the main beam and sometimes out of the back of the antenna as well. These don't usually make much difference,

but if you pass close to a very good reflector (such as a slab-sided metal ship) the blob on the screen that represents the ship may appear to grow until it forms a bright crescent-shape or even a full circle around the centre of the radar screen.

Receiver

The receiver's job is almost self-explanatory: it has to take the returning echoes that have been picked up by the antenna, and convert them into a form that can be used by the display. Microwave frequencies are tricky things to handle, however, so its first task is to reduce the super high frequency echoes to a more manageable level, referred to in radar specification sheets as the *intermediate frequency*.

The next stage of the process is to amplify the very weak returning signals. It's obvious, when you think about it, that the echoes received from targets at short range are likely to be very much stronger than those further away. A ship that is only a quarter of a mile away, for instance, will produce an echo that is over a million times stronger than the echo from an identical ship at eight miles. The amplifying circuitry has to cope with this huge range of signal strengths, and convert them all to a more or less equal level. In other words, at the instant after the transmitter has produced its pulse, the receiver starts listening for returning echoes with its amplification set to a fairly low level, but as the microseconds pass, it turns up its amplification in order to handle the progressively weaker echoes expected from more distant objects.

TR cell

The transmitters used by small craft radars are puny things compared with those in commercial and military radars, but they are still pretty powerful by comparison with anything else on board. Typically, we're talking about somewhere between 1500W and 5000W. Compare that with a domestic microwave cooker (700W), a VHF radio (25W) or a navigation light bulb (10W).

Their receivers, on the other hand, have to be very, very sensitive in order to detect the tiny whispers of radio energy that are returned as echoes from distant targets.

The effect of squirting several kilowatts of microwave energy straight into a hyper-sensitive receiver would be quick, catastrophic, and permanent.

To stop this happening, the radar has an electronic gate designed to isolate the receiver from the transmitter and antenna when the transmitter is actually transmitting. So far as radar technicians are concerned, there are several different ways of achieving this, but from the user's point of view they can all be lumped together under the general heading of **TR cell** (Transmit/Receive cell). The main significance of the TR cell is that the change-over from transmit to receive is not instantaneous, so a radar cannot be expected to detect objects at very close range. Most of the time, this doesn't present a problem, but it is worth remembering if, for instance, you are thinking of using radar to 'home in' on a buoy in thick fog, because the buoy will disappear from the radar screen about 20 or 30m before you hit it!

Display

It is up to the display to convert the fruits of all this frantic electronic activity into a form that is comprehensible to a human operator. The information can be presented in many different ways, but all small craft radars use a display format known as a **plan position indicator** – so called because the picture looks rather like a map or plan, portraying the vessel's surroundings as though you were looking down on the world from somewhere directly above the antenna.

There are still a few old-fashioned radars

around that use a radial scan cathode ray tube (see page 19), in which the beam of electrons from the electron gun is deflected by electromagnets, mounted outside the neck of the tube. The magnets rotate around the tube, in step with the rotating antenna so that the direction the beam is deflected corresponds to the direction the antenna is pointing at the time.

At the precise instant that the radar pulse is transmitted, a progressively increasing voltage is applied to the deflector magnets. If the electron gun were actually firing, this progressively increasing voltage would move the spot of light outwards from the centre of the screen towards its edge, in step with the progress of the radar pulse across the surface of the Earth. The electron gun, however, only fires when an echo is received, so it produces a spot of light on the screen whose distance from the centre corresponds with the range of the object that created the echo.

The overall result is that the display gradually builds up a picture made up of several thousand radial lines, each corresponding to a single transmitted pulse.

Advancing technology, however, has given us something known as a **raster scan** or **daylight viewing display**, in which a dedicated computer, built into the display unit, takes the range and bearing information provided by the receiver and antenna and converts it into 'X' and 'Y' co-ordinates, which it stores in its memory. The beauty of this is that within a few seconds of the first pulse being transmitted, the radar's memory contains all the data required to produce a picture on the screen, regularly updated as new information is received. Because the information is stored, the entire screen image can be refreshed many times a second, instead of once every three seconds. That, in turn, means that it's possible to use a conventional television or computer type screen, or a liquid crystal display.

Power consumption and safety

Widespread fears about the effects of exposure to electromagnetic radiation and the relatively high power quoted for even small radars inevitably causes concern to anyone thinking of installing or using a radar. Sailing yachtsmen, in particular, are also often worried about the effect that switching on a radar might have on their relatively limited supplies of electrical power.

Microwaves make up part of what is known as the electromagnetic spectrum. It spans such a huge range of wavelengths and frequencies, that the numbers involved are almost incomprehensible: suffice it to say that the now-defunct Omega navigation system, operating at wavelengths in the order of 30km, is almost at one end, while Gamma rays with wavelengths measurable in billionths of a millimetre are at the other.

Visible light is roughly in the middle of this vast spectrum, with a wavelength of about 600 millionths of a millimetre. Radar, with its wavelength of 3cm, is a long way below it.

It's pretty common knowledge that high frequency radiation can cause chemical changes in the body, which can cause (or cure) cancer and various genetic defects. Ultra violet light, certainly, has been blamed for causing skin cancer. Ordinary visible light, however, has no such effects, so it seems reasonable to assume that the very much lower frequencies used by radar are innocent – at least so far as that particular charge is concerned.

It's also a matter of common knowledge that microwaves can cook things by using radio energy to vibrate the molecules of the food placed inside it: it's this molecular activity that we recognise as 'heat'. There's no doubt that radar, operating at much the same frequency and at several times the power output of a domestic microwave, is potentially capable of cooking human tissue, especially the most vulnerable organs such as the eyes and genitals.

There are two saving graces. The first is that cookery, even in a microwave cooker, takes time. The pulses of energy emanating from a radar scanner are so short that they can't heat you up very much, so you have plenty of time between successive pulses to cool down again. The second is distance. Food, in a microwave cooker, is usually within about 10cm of the source of microwaves. At a distance of 20cm, the effective power is reduced by a factor of four: at 40cm it's down to one eighth, and so on.

It's possible – but very tedious – to work out the actual risk involved, but for practical purposes it is enough to appreciate that you expose yourself to considerably greater risk by using a mobile telephone or handheld VHF than by sitting next to a small craft radar, and that you would be hit on the head by the rotating scanner long before you got anywhere near the limits imposed by government health advice.

Still, a word of warning is in order: some Eastern European governments specify exposure limits that are a thousand times lower than our own, and it is quite possible that there may be health risks that haven't yet been discovered. To be on the safe side, it is good practice to avoid lingering in the beam of an operating radar and to avoid looking straight at the scanner.

A far greater risk is the relatively mundane risk of electric shock. Some parts of a radar operate at very high voltages indeed, and these voltages can persist even after the radar has been switched off or disconnected from the power supply. In normal use, the radar is perfectly safe, but you should never be tempted to take the back off it or remove any of the protective covers unless the instruction manual specifically tells you to.

12

Radar – getting a picture

A radar set may look complicated to the uninitiated, but that's only because many of the controls and the terminology involved are unfamiliar. There are, in fact, only about a dozen main controls that are standard to almost all marine radars – rather fewer than on a domestic stereo system or even a modern cooker!

Switching on and setting up

On-off and transmit-standby

The purpose of the **on-off** control is self evident: when the radar is switched off, it's completely dead. Switching it on supplies power to the display unit and scanner, getting the radar ready for use. It won't, however, be fully operational at once. Most modern radars begin by performing an automatic self-test procedure, and then show a rudimentary picture with the word 'wait' or a count-down timer in the centre.

The main reason for this is that the magnetron heats up as soon as it starts working. The sudden rise in temperature could be enough to damage it, so it's fitted with a heater to warm it up more gradually over a period of two or three minutes before it starts work. Some older models were fitted with a temperature sensor to tell you when they were ready, but nowadays it's more common to use an automatic timer instead. Once the magnetron is ready, or sufficient time has elapsed, the set switches itself into **standby** mode. At this stage, the radar is all ready to use, but it isn't actually transmitting. To get a picture, you need to

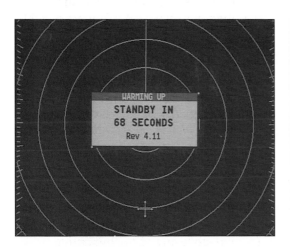

When the power is switched on, the radar goes into an automatic self-test and warm-up procedure, with a count-down timer on screen.

At the end of the warm-up procedure, the radar switches to standby mode, ready for use, but not transmitting.

switch the transmitter on – usually by pressing a button marked 'Tx' or 'X-mit'.

It's always possible to switch back into standby: this saves power by stopping the transmitter, but leaves the magnetron heater switched on so that the radar is ready for immediate use.

Brilliance and contrast

Even while the radar is in standby mode, you can begin adjusting it to suit your own preferences and the prevailing conditions by adjusting the **brilliance** control. This has much the same effect as the corresponding control on a domestic television: it makes the picture brighter for use in strong sunlight, or dimmer for use at night.

LCD displays also have a **contrast** control which may need to be adjusted as well to suit the lighting conditions and the angle at which you are looking at the screen.

Gain

Unlike the brilliance and contrast controls, which only affect the display, the **gain** control has a fundamental effect on the radar receiver, so it can only be adjusted when the radar is actually transmitting.

It's similar, in many respects, to the squelch control on a VHF radio, because it adjusts the receiver sensitivity. If the gain is set too low, weak echoes will be lost, but if it is too high, the screen will be filled with a mass of speckles – the visual equivalent of the hissing and crackling noise you hear on a VHF if the squelch is wrongly adjusted.

The aim of the adjustment is to make the receiver as sensitive as possible without the 'snowstorm' effect, so the best way to achieve it is to turn the gain control up until it is obviously too high, and then turn it down until the speckles disappear. Some operators like to leave a faint background speckle, and on a radial scan display or an exceptionally good quality raster display there is a lot to be said for this approach.

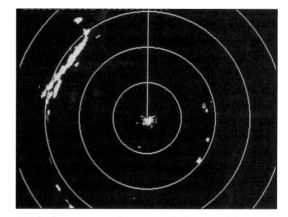

With the gain too low, very little is visible on the screen.

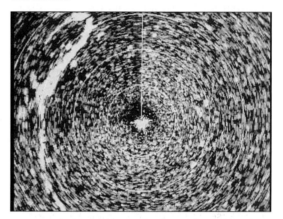

Turning the gain up too high produces a 'blizzard' of radio noise.

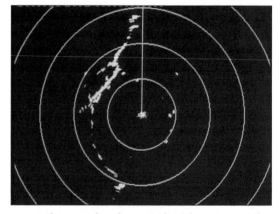

Now, the gain has been reduced to remove the excess noise, and the range increased ready to begin tuning.

On most small craft raster displays, how-ever, there is a risk that an individual speckle may be big enough to hide a real contact.

Range

The effect and purpose of the range con-trol, too, is reasonably self evident: it enlarges or reduces the scale of the picture on the screen. On the shortest range scale, for instance, the distance from the centre of the picture to the edge may represent as little as one eighth of a nautical mile, increasing to 16 miles or 24 miles or even more on the maximum range. It's not unusual for big commercial radars to offer range scales up to 120 miles!

Different range scales suit different pur-poses. To monitor progress on an offshore passage, you may well want to use a long range scale, to see distant coastlines. For collision avoidance, it is better to choose a medium scale, such as six or twelve miles, while for inshore pilotage it may be neces-sary to go down to a mile or less.

Whilst the effect on the picture is usually obvious, it's worth bearing in mind that the range control also changes the pulse length and pulse repetition frequency, so a short range scale gives better discrimination than a long one.

Tuning

Like any radio receiver, the radar's receiver needs to be tuned to match the frequency of the transmitter. In the case of a radar, always listening for echoes of its own trans-missions, it might seem that a tuning control is redundant, and that it should be possible for it to be set up in the factory and then left alone. In practice, however, that isn't possible. The exact frequency of the magnetron's transmissions varies slightly, depending mainly on its operating temperature: it tends to drop slightly in the first half hour after the radar is switched on, and to rise slightly if the outside air

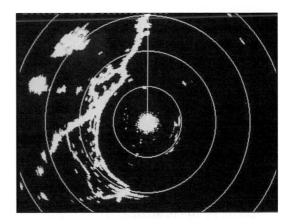

Careful tuning produces this picture, in which the coastline is clearly visible on the left, with Dungeness now visible near the bottom of the picture, and Dover near the top. Several ships can be seen, including two (in the top right-hand corner) that are about 15 miles away.

temperature drops – at night, for instance. Bearing in mind that the receiver is listen-ing for very weak echoes indeed, it makes sense to give it the best possible chance by fine tuning it to compensate for these small variations.

If possible, the best way to adjust the tuning is to set the radar to a range some-where in the upper half of the choice of scales available. For most small boat radars, that's usually something in the order of 12 miles. Look for a weak contact somewhere near the outer edge of the screen, and adjust the tuning in small steps, until the contact looks as big, bright, and strong as possible.

Take your time: remember that on most radars the scanner rotates at about 20–25 rpm, so it could take up to 3 seconds for any change you make to take effect. You may find that adjusting the tuning turns a weak contact into a strong one: if so, look around to see if you can find a weak con-tact that wasn't visible before, and turn your attention to that.

If there are no real contacts visible at all,

it may be possible to tune the radar using the echoes returned from waves: to do this, though, you will need to choose a much shorter range scale than would normally be the case, so the results may not be as good.

Many radars have a 'tuning indicator' in the form of a little bar graph on the screen. An easy short cut is to adjust the tuning control until the tuning indicator shows its maximum. Whilst this can be guaranteed to produce a reasonably good result, it is seldom quite as effective as tuning by eye.

Basic set-up procedure

In the days of radial scan radars, it became accepted 'best practice' amongst professional radar operators to turn all the main operating controls – especially the brilliance – fully anticlockwise before switching the set off, and to carry out the entire switching on procedure from scratch every time.

On a raster scan radar, such precautions are unnecessary, but it is still worth getting into the habit of going through a standard start-up routine every time you switch a radar on. It's not difficult to remember: apart from the on-off-standby-transmit control, the other four (or five) controls need to be adjusted in alphabetical order:

- Brilliance

- Contrast (LCD radars only)

- Gain

- Range

- Tune

Many radars offer automatic gain and tune controls. In some ways, they can be compared with the settings on an automatic camera, in that they virtually guarantee that anyone can get a reasonable picture. A reasonably skilled operator, however, will always get a better result by using the manual controls, especially in less-than-perfect conditions.

Improving the picture

The controls we've covered so far are all fundamental to the business of getting a picture on the radar screen. The next group are involved in improving the picture by adapting it to suit particular conditions.

Sea clutter

Sea clutter is the name given to a mass of speckles around the centre of the screen that can sometimes be caused by radar

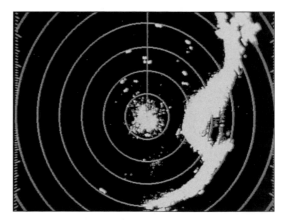

The mass of clutter at the centre of this screen is caused by echoes from the surface of the sea.

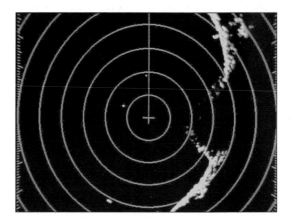

In this picture, the sea clutter control has got rid of the sea clutter, but it has been overdone: all the small craft and much of the land echoes have been obliterated.

pulses being reflected from the surface of the sea itself. In calm or smooth waters, this isn't a problem, but as the sea gets rougher the area affected increases, and the clutter can strengthen to such an extent that it obscures the echoes from solid objects such as buoys and small vessels.

Antenna height makes a difference to the seriousness of the sea clutter problem. For a low antenna, the faces of distant waves are obscured by those that are close at hand, so sea clutter may be confined to a radius of a few hundred metres. At the other extreme, large ships, whose radar scanners may be mounted thirty metres or more above the waterline, quite often suffer sea clutter extending out to four miles or more.

The sea clutter control is sometimes labelled 'anti-clutter sea' or occasionally 'swept gain' or 'STC' (for 'sensitivity time control'). Whatever its name, it works on the basis that sea clutter only occurs at relatively short range. The control gets rid of sea clutter by reducing the receiver gain for the first few microseconds after each pulse has been transmitted, then gradually restores it to its normal level.

The snag with this is that all close-range echoes are affected. The radar cannot know whether a particular echo comes from a buoy, boat, or even from a ship or a piece of coastline: if it's at short range, it will be weakened by the sea clutter control, and possibly removed from the screen altogether.

The sea clutter control has been described as the most dangerous knob on a radar set, so it pays to treat it like chilli powder in cookery: a little can make a world of difference, but too much defeats the whole object!

Rain clutter

Rain clutter, as its name suggests, is clutter caused by rain – or, to a lesser extent, by sleet, hail, or snow. It almost goes without

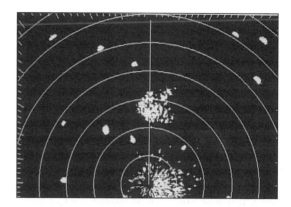

The bright patch in the centre of the picture (above the centre of the screen) is caused by echoes from rain or clouds.

saying that an individual raindrop or hailstone is much too small to produce a discernible echo by itself. A mass of them, however, is capable of reflecting quite a significant amount of energy.

On screen, the effect is often described as producing a 'cotton wool' echo. That's a valid description on an old-fashioned radial scan display, but on a raster scan radar, rain clutter looks very much more granular – a mass of speckles, like those of sea clutter, but not necessarily concentrated around the centre of the display.

The fact that rain clutter can occur anywhere on the screen means that the sea clutter control can't be used to get rid of it. Fortunately, however, the nature of the echo is such that a different weapon can be used to combat it.

Like the sea clutter control, the rain clutter control rejoices in several different names – 'anti-clutter rain', 'differentiation', 'fast time constant', or 'FTC'. Whatever you call it, the rain clutter control works on the basis that the echo from a patch of rain is likely to be weaker but more drawn-out than the echo from a solid target. By cutting off all but the leading edge of each returning echo, the rain clutter circuit reduces most rain echoes to such an extent

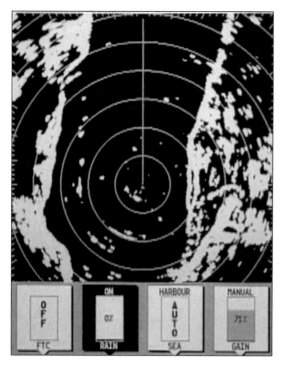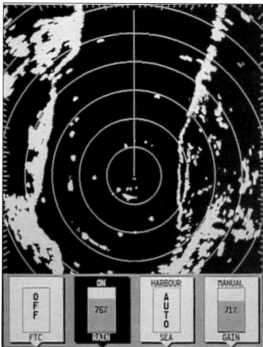

This radar is slightly unusual in having a fully adjustable rain clutter control. Notice that even when turned up high, it has relatively little effect on the steep and solid coastline on the left-hand side. On the right, low-lying salt marshes give a very weak echo when the rain clutter control is switched on.

that they are too weak to appear on the display at all. Even the strongest will be reduced to a thin line, instead of a solid smudge, so targets which might have been hidden inside the rain area become visible.

Unlike the sea clutter control, which is usually progressive – so it can be set to any level between fully 'on' and fully 'off' – the rain clutter control of most small boat radars is either 'on' or not, with nothing in between. Progressive control isn't really necessary, because the rain clutter control is generally far less dangerous than its sea clutter counterpart.

One particular type of 'genuine' echo, though, can be significantly affected by it. Low-lying, gently-sloping coastlines generally produce relatively weak, drawn out echoes, which show up on screen as a thick but often rather diffuse contact. They are affected by the rain clutter control in just the same way as rain clutter; with the trailing edge of the echo cut off, they appear as a much thinner, and sometimes broken, line.

Interference rejection

Watching television or listening to the radio, we've all come across the phenomenon of interference, in which the signal we are trying to receive is partly obscured by another strong but unwanted signal.

Although all X-band radars operate at about the same frequency and wavelength as each other, manufacturing tolerances on their magnetrons are deliberately loose enough to allow the exact frequency to vary by up to 200MHz. Just for comparison, the entire range of international marine VHF channels fit into just 6MHz.

To a large extent, then, the risk of interference from other radars is reduced by an element of chance: there aren't likely to be many vessels around that are transmitting on the same frequency as each other. Even so, the sensitivity of a radar's receiver means that radar interference can be a problem, especially in crowded areas such as the English Channel.

The classic effect of radar interference from a single radar transmitting on a frequency very similar to your own is a pattern of dotted lines, radiating outwards like curved spokes, or like the sparks of a catherine wheel. Nowadays, however, you're more likely to see the cumulative effect of a lot of radars on a slightly wider spread of frequencies. Unfortunately, it's nowhere near as pretty – just a mass of bright spots or speckles, sometimes making up short lengths of dotted line, but more often appearing as a random mess.

Fortunately, the technological advances that made radar really popular – and that might therefore be blamed for making the problem worse – have also given us the solution in what is known as 'line-to-line correlation'. In effect, the radar's computer compares the picture that it is about to send to the screen with the one before. If there is a speck on the new picture that wasn't there in the previous one, the computer assumes that it must be interference.

Real contacts, in other words, show up because they appear twice in the same place, but interference doesn't.

Compared with the dangers of the clutter controls, interference rejection is pretty innocuous, with so few drawbacks that many users leave it switched on all the time, and some manufacturers give you no choice in the matter. It does, however, tend to reduce the appearance of the background speckle which is so important in adjusting the gain control, so it's not a bad idea to switch the interference rejection off when you're switching on and setting up the radar.

It's also often said that IR hides radar beacons (racons, see page 104). That's true, but only up to a point: it could hide *certain types of* racons, but these are extremely rare.

Stabilisation

Until a few years ago, the vast majority of small craft radars were what is known as 'head-up, relative motion' sets. Nowadays, however, most models offer a variety of alternative display modes, each with its own advantages and drawbacks.

Head-up

On the most basic marine radar display, your own vessel is always at the centre of the screen and heading straight upwards. A bright line called the Ship's Head Marker (SHM) or Heading Mark (HM) identifies the straight-ahead position.

Aside from the fact that it is relatively cheap and simple, the big virtue of a head-up display is that the picture on the screen corresponds very closely with what you see from the cockpit or wheelhouse: objects ahead of the boat appear at the top of the display, objects astern appear at the bottom, objects on the port side appear on the left-hand side of the screen, and so on. The corresponding drawback is that when you alter course, the picture appears to rotate. If the boat is yawing, this can make large contacts appear to 'smear' around the screen, while making any small or weak contacts disappear. It can also make it very difficult to measure bearings accurately.

North-up

On all but the most basic models, it's possible to overcome most of these problems by linking the radar to an electronic compass. Software inside the radar can then turn the

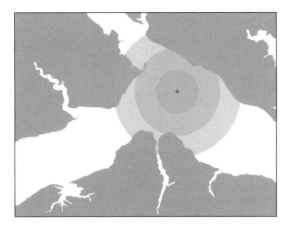

picture round to put north at the top of the screen.

On a north-up display, your own vessel is still at the centre of the picture with its heading represented by the SHM. The screen image, however, doesn't necessarily correspond directly with what you can see. If you are heading south, for instance, the SHM points downwards, so targets on the port side of the boat appear as contacts on the right-hand side of the display.

One virtue of the north-up mode is that the orientation of the screen picture

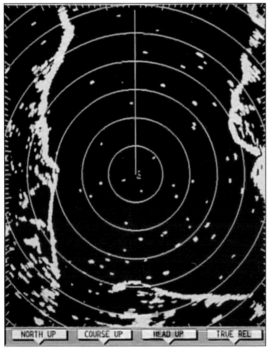

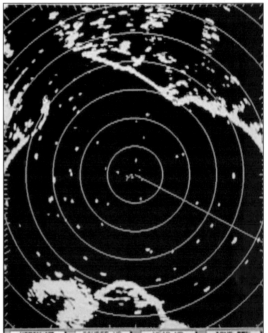

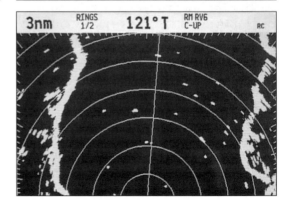

Fig 40 (Top) Compare this sketch map of the central Solent with the radar pictures below it.
Above left: Head-up: our boat is steering approximately 120 degrees, so the Isle of Wight (at the bottom of Fig 40) is in the right-hand side of the screen.
Above right: North-up: we are still steering 120 degrees, but the radar has rotated the picture 120 degrees anticlockwise, so it can be compared directly with the chart.
Right: Course-up: notice that although the picture is similar to a head-up radar, the heading mark is not upright.

matches that of a standard navigational chart, making it particularly useful when you are using the radar for navigation or pilotage rather than for collision avoidance. The other is that fixed objects don't appear to swing around the screen as they do in a head-up display. The corresponding disadvantage is that many people find it more difficult to compare what they see on a north-up radar with what they see by looking around them.

A few radars have been produced that offer a similar facility called *south-up*. It's effect is obvious, but its benefits are limited because no-one that I know of produces south-up charts!

Course-up

Course-up mode, in some respects, offers the best of both worlds. It uses a compass interfaced to the radar to stabilise the picture by counteracting the effect of yawing, but instead of putting north at the top, it lives up to its name by putting your course upwards. The picture, overall, looks very much like that of a head-up display, except that the image is more stable, and any yawing is indicated by the heading mark wobbling from side to side of its straight-up position rather than by fixed objects appearing to move.

This makes course-up particularly good for collision avoidance, so long as the course selected on the radar really does represent the course you are steering. Neither the heading sensor nor the radar can tell the difference between a short-term accidental yaw and a long-term intentional alteration of course, so it is up to the radar operator to remember to re-set the course-up mode whenever the boat has altered course. In most cases, setting a new course is a simple matter of switching to one of the other modes, and then switching back to course up: the radar takes its new course to be whatever your heading was at the moment you engaged course-up.

Off-centring

Off-centring allows the centre of the radar picture to be moved away from the centre of the screen. It's most useful on fast boats, because it allows you to look further ahead without reducing the scale of the picture: you can, for instance, look nine miles ahead and three miles astern whilst keeping the radar switched to its six-mile range scale. Zoom has a somewhat similar effect, in that it enlarges a portion of the radar picture.

True motion

True motion is a very sophisticated refinement of off-centring, in which the centre of the radar picture automatically moves across the screen in step with the boat's progress across the real world.

To achieve this, the radar needs to be linked either to an accurate log and compass (known as 'sea-stabilised true motion') or to a reliable position fixer such as GPS (known as 'ground-stabilised true motion'). Its effect is that objects which are stationary in the real world should appear as stationary contacts on the screen, while the movement of contacts on the screen is a reasonably accurate representation of the movement of the corresponding objects in real life.

It has been used on warships for many years, and is becoming increasingly common on large civilian vessels, but for small craft it sounds much better than it really is. Spotting collision risks, in particular, is very much more difficult on a true motion display than on a relative motion display.

Measuring tools

The classic radar picture, familiar from countless films and TV programmes, has a conspicuous pattern of concentric rings equally spaced around its centre and a somewhat less obvious scale of degrees around the outside edge.

The scale of degrees is intended to help the radar observer estimate bearings rather more accurately than would be possible by eye alone.

The rings serve much the same purpose, but are concerned with range instead of bearing. Their number and spacing varies, depending on the make and model of radar and the range scale in use: you may find, for instance, that on a six-mile setting, there may be six rings at one mile intervals, or that on a 16-mile range setting there may be four rings, four miles apart. The spacing will be shown somewhere on the display, usually in a little data box in one corner.

If you don't want the rings – if you don't like them, or are worried that a range ring might hide some small but important contact – they can always be switched off by pressing the 'rings off' button (or its counterpart in a menu control system).

The heading mark, too, can be deleted, though not in quite the same way. Pressing the 'HM delete' button certainly removes the heading mark, but it will come back again as soon as you release the button. This is a hang-on from the world of commercial shipping, where it is occasionally useful to delete the heading mark in order to check that it isn't obscuring a small contact. In small craft radars, it's a pretty pointless facility: the beamwidth of a small radar is unlikely to produce a contact small enough to hide behind the heading mark, and in any case it would take a helmsman of quite remarkable skill to steer accurately enough to keep the contact hidden by the heading mark for more than a few seconds at a time!

Electronic bearing line

The scale of bearings marked around the edge of the picture is useful, but is nowhere near accurate enough for most navigation purposes, so almost all radars have at least one electronic bearing line (EBL).

In its most basic form, an EBL consists of a line similar to the heading mark, but which can be swept around the display by means of a control on the front panel of the radar. To take a bearing of a particular contact, you simply move the EBL until it cuts through the contact in question, and then read the bearing from the EBL data box on the screen.

Whilst many navigators who have been brought up with traditional methods are quite happy to use the EBL as a sort of high-tech hand bearing compass, its use does require some caution and it is always important to remember that measuring bearings is not radar's strongest suit:

- If the heading mark has not been correctly adjusted so that it accurately represents the fore-and-aft line of the boat, then all the bearings taken with the radar will be wrong by the same amount.

- The beamwidth of the radar tends to make contacts look bigger than they should, especially if they are good reflectors or at short range. In the case of small targets, such as buoys and beacons, this effect can be overcome by making the EBL cut through the centre of the contact. For larger objects, such as islands and headlands, the effect can be minimised by making the EBL cut just inside the edge of the contact, by an amount equal to half the beamwidth.

- On a head-up display, any bearing measured by the radar will be relative to the heading mark. An object on the port beam, for instance, will be shown as bearing 270°. For most purposes, this will have to be converted to a true bearing before it is of any use.

Converting relative bearings to true

In principle, converting relative bearings to true is a simple matter of adding your heading to the relative bearing.

In most cases, the biggest error is in the

heading: you need to know exactly where the boat was pointing at the moment you set the EBL on the contact. In practice, this requires close co-operation between the helmsman and the radar operator. The snag is that few helmsmen can actually steer as accurately as they like to think they can!

Having established the actual heading, the calculation goes like this:

Relative	eg	296° (R)	bearing shown on display
+ Heading	eg	157° (C)	from steering compass
= Compass bearing		453° (C)	
± Deviation		006° E	add easterly or subtract westerly (see note[4])
= Magnetic bearing		459° (M)	
± Variation		004° W	from chart (add easterly or subtract westerly)
= True bearing		455° (T)	
− 360°		360°	if necessary, to give an answer less than 360°
		095° (T)	

The calculation is straightforward enough, but it involves so many stages that it's easy to make a mistake. If you need to take several bearings in quick succession, the chances of making a mistake are multiplied.

If the radar is operating in north-up mode, the bearings it provides are usually referred to the compass that is supplying heading information to the radar, so you don't need to make the conversion from ° Relative to ° Compass. If the compass is uncorrected, however, you will still have to apply variation and deviation. At the other extreme, if the compass has automatic deviation and variation correction, you may not have to make any extra corrections at all, so it's important to know exactly what you are dealing with.

Variable range marker

The variable range marker (VRM, or range strobe) is an extra range ring. Unlike the pattern of fixed rings, however, it can be enlarged or contracted by a control on

the radar's front panel, and its radius is shown in a data box on the screen. To measure the range of a target, you enlarge the VRM until it appears to just brush the edge of the relevant contact.

Radar ranges aren't immune from errors, but they are inherently more accurate than bearing measurements, and there is no need for any of the mathematical jiggery-pokery that has to be applied to radar bearings.

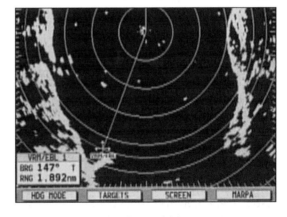

The variable range marker (VRM) and electronic bearing line (EBL) in use, to measure the range and bearing of a conspicuous jetty. Many radars (including this one) use a single cursor control to adjust the VRM and EBL simultaneously.

Floating EBL and VRM

It is becoming increasingly common for radars to be equipped with two or more EBLs and VRMs. In some cases, the extra

[4]The deviation figure varies from boat to boat, from compass to compass, and from heading to heading: it should be the figure appropriate to the boat's heading at the time the bearing was taken and for the compass in use.

VRM and EBL are able to 'float', so that their centre can be put anywhere on the screen. There are all sorts of potential uses for this: if you are trying to pick out a small buoy or boat, for instance, and you know its range and bearing from a conspicuous headland, you might use the floating VRM and EBL to mark where the contact should be on your screen.

Cursor

On old-fashioned radial-scan radars, the word 'cursor' is used to refer to a glass or plastic disc with a pattern of straight lines engraved on it. It could be rotated, to serve exactly the same purpose as the EBL of a raster scan radar.

Nowadays, however, the term is more often used in the same sense as on a computer screen: it means a mark such as a small cross or circle that can be moved around the screen by means of a joystick or tracker ball. The cursor can serve all sorts of purposes: it may be used to determine where the centre of an off-centred picture is to be, to 'anchor' a floating EBL or VRM, or to set up a guard zone (see page 119). In most cases, however, its range and bearing from the centre of the picture appears in a data box on screen, so you can use it as a kind of combined EBL and VRM to measure the range and bearing of a target simultaneously.

13

Radar – what shows up?

Even when you've got the best picture your radar can possibly achieve, there will still be some things that won't show up, and perhaps one or two things that appear on the screen even though they don't exist in the real world. These aren't faults, any more than our inability to see through brick walls or in total darkness suggests that there is anything wrong with our eyesight.

The fundamental point is that in order to produce an echo, a target must first be struck by some of the microwave energy from the radar, and must then be able to reflect it back to the antenna. Various things can conspire to stop this from happening:

Blind arcs and shadow sectors

It's pretty obvious that an obstruction on board the boat, such as a funnel, may block the radar's transmissions, causing a blind arc. Slightly less obvious is the fact that a smaller obstruction – such as a sailing boat's mast – will cut out some of the radar energy, to produce a shadow sector, in which the radar's ability to detect small objects or weak reflectors is reduced.

Small craft, in general, don't suffer from blind arcs, and their shadow sectors are very much less significant than those caused by the cargo handling gear of merchant ships, but if you have a particular problem – such as a very small antenna mounted on the spreaders of a large mast, it may be worth making up a shadow

diagram to show the affected areas, and sticking it somewhere near the radar display as a reminder.

There are various ways of doing this, but the simplest approach is to find a patch of slightly choppy water. With the sea clutter control turned right down, select a range scale that is short enough to show a distinct circle of sea clutter on the screen, and note any areas in which the sea clutter is significantly less noticeable than others (shadow sectors) or in which it is absent altogether (blind arcs).

Shadow areas

Shadow areas are very, very much more common than shadow sectors or blind arcs, because they are caused by large obstructions outside the boat – most commonly by the coastline itself. Islands or headlands can block the radar's view of a more distant stretch of coastline just as they hide them from the naked eye.

There's nothing you can do about this, other than to appreciate that it happens.

Radar horizon

The biggest obstruction of all is the Earth itself, whose curvature limits our own eyesight by creating a visual horizon. It has much the same effect on radar. The radar horizon is very slightly further away than the visual horizon, because radar waves are slightly bent by passing through the atmosphere, but the radar horizon is still surprisingly close. (See Fig 42.)

For most practical purposes, you can work it out by using the *Distance to sea*

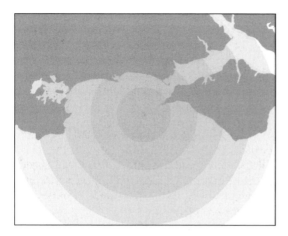

Fig 41 *A sketch map of the area shown in the radar image below.*

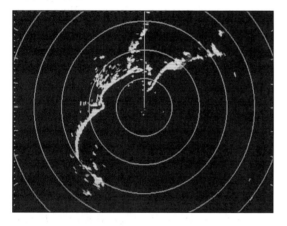

This head-up picture is skewed about 45 degrees anticlockwise compared with the corresponding map in Fig 41. Anvil Point (bottom left) looks more like a cluster of islands, because the low-lying ground to the north is hidden below the radar horizon. The Solent (top right) is hidden behind the Isle of Wight.

horizon tables that are included in yachtsmen's almanacs, or from the formula $D = 2.2 \times \sqrt{H_a}$, in which D is the distance to the radar horizon in nautical miles, and H_a is the antenna height in metres.

For an antenna mounted 4m above the waterline, for instance, the radar horizon is only 4.4 miles away:

$$D = 2.2 \times \sqrt{4}$$
$$= 2.2 \times 2$$
$$= 4.4$$

Based on this formula, it is also possible to calculate the greatest possible distance at which you could possibly expect to see a distant coastline on radar, just as you might use the sea horizon tables to work out the visible range of a lighthouse.

Suppose, for instance, that you have a radar mounted 4m above the waterline, and that you are hoping to see a cliff that is 100m high. Your radar horizon is 4.4 miles.

For a radar mounted on top of the cliff, the horizon would be 22 miles away:

$$D = 2.2 \times \sqrt{100}$$
$$= 2.2 \times 10$$
$$= 22$$

So if the two radars were sufficiently powerful and sensitive, they would be able to see each other at a range of 26.4 miles.

It's worth noticing that this formula doesn't include the power or nominal range of the radar: the answer is the same for a radar whose nominal range is 36 miles as for one that is sold as a 72-mile set. Powerful radars have their advantages, but being able to see over the horizon is not one of them!

The other interesting point is that although you can certainly increase the effective range of a radar, by mounting the

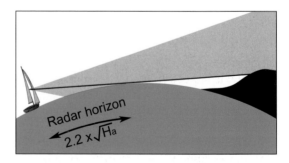

Fig 42 *The radar's view is limited by the horizon.*

scanner higher up, the benefits of doing so are generally slight.

Suppose, for instance, that we increased the scanner height to 9m. Its radar horizon would be increased to 6.6 miles:

$$D = 2.2 \times \sqrt{9}$$
$$= 2.2 \times 3$$
$$= 6.6$$

The radar horizon from the clifftop would still be 22 miles, so the maximum range at which the cliff might be expected to appear on the radar would be 28.6 miles.

More than doubling the antenna height, in other words, has only increased the radar's effective range by a couple of miles. At the same time, it has increased the extent of sea clutter, and will have put the scanner unit out of reach of any maintenance man who is armed only with a typical boatyard ladder.

What shows up?

Even if it is illuminated by the radar beam, an object which does not return at least some of the microwave energy towards the antenna will be invisible to radar. Five factors determine whether a target will reflect radar pulses or not:

• Material

• Size

• Aspect

• Texture

• Shape

Material
Material is important because some materials (such as GRP) are effectively transparent to microwaves, while others (such as wood) absorb them. Materials which are good conductors of electricity absorb the microwaves but immediately re-radiate them. In other words, for most practical purposes we can say that conductive materials are good reflectors.

Size
The effect of size is almost self-evident: a very big object will occupy more of the radar beam, so it will absorb – and re-radiate – more of the transmitted energy than a smaller one made of the same material

Aspect, texture, and shape
Aspect, texture, and shape are closely related to each other, and can be visualised by thinking of the radar scanner as though it were a torch, while the target is represented by a mirror.

If the mirror is at right angles to the approaching beam, the energy will be reflected straight back the way it came. If, however, the mirror is angled very slightly away, then the reflected beam will be deflected. In radar terms, the pulse would be reflected, but it wouldn't be returned to the scanner.

To see the effect of **texture**, imagine that the mirror has been broken and rather carelessly reassembled, or that it is made from metal foil that has been screwed up and then roughly flattened. Even if it is not perfectly lined up at 90° to the beam, there's a good chance that some of its many facets will return some energy the way it came. In radar terms, a rough surface may not be quite as good a reflector as a smooth one, but it's a lot more reliable.

Shape is very much like texture, but on a larger scale. A flat-sided target, for instance, can be visualised as four vertical mirrors, so it can be expected to produce a strong echo so long as the radar beam strikes one of the sides at right angles. Seen from one corner, however, it will be a poor reflector because it is bouncing the echo away in the wrong direction.

A sphere, on the other hand, will always present part of its surface at right angles to the beam. Unfortunately, it will only be a tiny spot, while most of its surface area scatters the microwaves, rather than reflecting them, so its reflection will be weak but

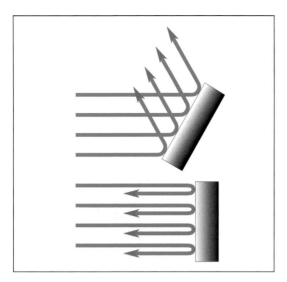

Fig 43 *Flat surfaces are generally good reflectors, but may bounce the radar energy away in the wrong direction.*

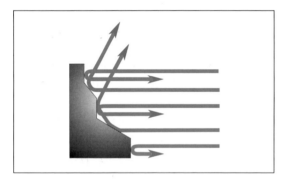

Fig 44 *Rough-textured surfaces generally give weaker but more consistent echoes.*

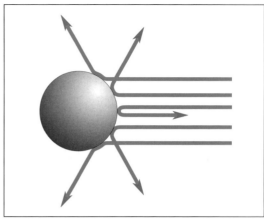

Fig 45 *Curved surfaces are generally poor reflectors: they tend to scatter the radar energy.*

can usually expect to see them at ranges of at least eight miles or so, and often considerably more. Buoys and small craft, by comparison, are poor reflectors. To overcome this problem, they are often fitted with devices known as radar reflectors[5].

There are many different designs, and competition between radar reflector manufacturers is fierce, but in general they can be classified into three distinct groups: octohedrals, stacked arrays, and lenses.

Octohedrals

Octohedrals are made up of interlocking plates of reflective material – usually sheets

[5]Under the requirements of the Safety of Life at Sea Convention (SOLAS), all vessels of less than 150 tons (whether used for commercial purposes or not) are required to carry a radar reflector when proceeding to sea.

reliable, regardless of where the beam is coming from or whether the sphere has been tilted or rolled.

Radar reflectors

As the table (right) shows, land and ships are generally very good reflectors of radar waves, so even on the smallest and least powerful yacht radar, you

	Land	Ships	Buoys	Boats
Material	Good	Excellent	Excellent	Poor
Size	Excellent	Good	Poor	Poor
Orientation	Varies	Varies	Varies	Varies
Shape	Varies	Fair	Poor	Poor
Texture	Good	Good	Poor	Poor
Overall	Very good	Very good	Quite poor	Poor

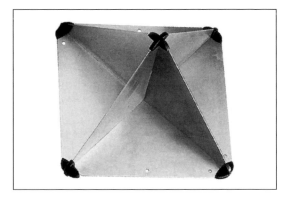

A classic 'octohedral' reflector, seen here in its correct 'catch-rain' position.

of aluminium alloy, though some types use a fine wire mesh laminated into GRP, and some even use metalised fabric stretched inside an inflatable outer casing. It's easy to visualise how they work if you think of the radar energy as though it were a squash ball being smacked into the corner of the court. No matter how the microwaves approach the corner between the reflective plates, they must eventually come out the way they went in. Octohedrals are cheap, light, simple, and reasonably effective so long as their plates are perfectly flat and perpendicular to each other, and so long as they are correctly mounted in the 'catch-rain' position.

Stacked arrays

Stacked arrays are more complex in design and construction and are usually enclosed within a cylindrical plastic casing, but the principle is similar: they consist of an arrangement of metal plates designed to form a number of corners which will reflect radar energy in the same way as those of an octohedral. (See Fig 46.)

Lens reflectors

Lens reflectors consist of a sphere of a special plastic compound which refracts radar waves in just the same way as a glass lens refracts light, combined with a metallic strip or coating. The plastic lens focusses the incoming radar energy onto the strip or coating, which reflects it: the reflected microwaves then pass back through the

Radar cross section

Legislators, engineers, and salesmen sometimes need to quantify how well something reflects radar waves. To do it, they usually refer to something known as its radar cross section (RCS) or its equivalent echoing area (EEA).

The RCS or EEA of something is an indication of how much radar energy it reflects when compared with a metal sphere with a cross section of 1 square metre. In other words, a radar reflector described as having an RCS of 10sqm will reflect as much radar energy as a sphere whose cross section is 10sqm and whose diameter must therefore be just over 3.5m.

A 3.5m metal ball sounds pretty big, but it's important to remember that a sphere produces a consistent response, but not a strong response. For a normal X-band radar, a metal plate just half the size of this book would have a comparable RCS, so long as it was absolutely perpendicular to the approaching radar beam.

In practice, the RCS of almost every real target varies quite significantly, depending on its orientation, so a single RCS figure is of pretty limited value: it could be a maximum figure, a minimum figure, or any of several different kinds of average. To overcome this problem, and to show how the RCS of a radar reflector varies as it is pitched, rolled, and rotated, radar cross section information is often presented in the form of graphs or diagrams.

lens which forms them back into a beam heading straight back the way they came.

Fig 46 *A polar diagram of a popular stacked array reflector, showing the characteristic peaks and troughs of response, depending on the angle from which the radar beam approaches it. Bear in mind that most of the peaks are roughly comparable with a flat metal plate the size of a compact disc.*

Radar transponders

Radar transponders represent a very different solution to the problem of making small targets more conspicuous to radar, because instead of trying to reflect the radar pulse, they respond to it by transmitting a distinctive return signal of their own.

Racons

Racons are used on navigation marks to draw attention to them and to help identify them. There are several different types of racons, but their common feature is that they respond to an incoming pulse by transmitting a longer and stronger pulse, on the same frequency. On the radar display of the vessel which transmitted the trigger

pulse, this appears as a long 'flash' on the radar screen. It looks a bit like an exclamation mark: the dot, nearest the centre of the screen, represents the racon structure itself while the stalk, radiating outward from the centre, represents its signal. In many cases, the racon signal is coded so that its flash is broken up, on screen, to form the pattern of dots and dashes of a Morse code letter.

Most racons are what is known as 'slow sweep'. They don't attempt to respond to pulses from several different radars all at once, but instead sweep relatively slowly across the range of frequencies used by marine radars. It usually takes a minute or two for a racon to wind itself up from 9.3GHz to 9.5GHz, before dropping back to 9.3GHz to start the process again. The result of this is that a racon won't show up

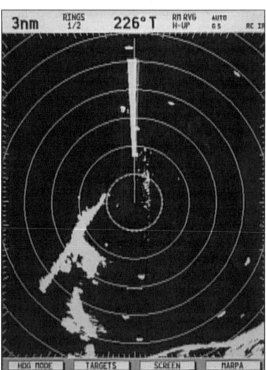

A racon is an active transponder, producing the distinctive 'flash' seen in the top centre of this radar screen.

on every sweep of your radar. It will start to appear as soon as its frequency is somewhere near that of your radar, and will gradually strengthen over the next sweep or two before fading away again.

Advancing technology has given us another kind of racon known as 'frequency agile'. As its name suggests, a frequency-agile racon jumps from frequency to frequency as necessary to respond to whatever radars are operating within range of it. So far as small craft radars are concerned, the effect of an agile frequency racon is almost exactly the same as that of a slow-sweep racon.

SARTs

A relatively new application of racon technology is in Search and Rescue Transponders, intended primarily to make liferafts more conspicuous to potential rescuers. The way they work is similar to the other types of racon, in that they transmit only when they receive a pulse from a radar. A SART transmission, however, is distinctive in that it produces a string of 12 dots equally spaced over a distance of about seven miles.

Radar target enhancers (RTEs)

Radar target enhancers are sometimes used instead of passive reflectors on yachts and other small craft. The basic principle is similar to a frequency agile racon, except that instead of producing a long pulse, a tiny fraction of a second after the trigger pulse is received, it transmits a look-alike pulse, virtually instantaneously. To anyone looking at the radar screen of the transmitting vessel, the idea is that an RTE signal should look exactly like the echo received from a conventional passive reflector, but stronger and more consistent.

False echoes

Radar operators are understandably concerned about things that might not show up on the radar screen because they don't reflect radar energy or because they are hidden below the horizon or beyond obstructions.

It's as well to be aware, however, of the fact that radar can occasionally be fooled into indicating the presence of objects that don't really exist, just as our eyes can be fooled by reflections and mirages. Fortunately, most of these false echoes are rare and short lived.

Indirect echoes

Indirect echoes arise when the radar pulses strike a good reflector and are bounced off in a different direction. If they then hit another target, and make the return trip, the radar will detect the echo produced by the real target, but will 'see' it in the wrong direction. Usually (but not invariably), indirect echoes that are caused by reflections from objects onboard your own vessel appear in shadow sectors or blind arcs. Indirect echoes caused by objects outside your own vessel (such as large ships nearby or steel shuttering on a sea wall) appear in places where real contacts are obviously impossible.

One rare but potentially worrying 'special case' can arise when approaching a steel bridge. If the bridge itself acts as a good reflector, there is a possibility that you will see your own echo on the radar screen, apparently heading towards the same part of the bridge, but from the opposite direction.

Multiple echoes are another 'special case' variation of indirect echoes, which can arise when two steel vessels are close to each other, so that the radar pulses bounce backwards and forwards between the two vessels. It's rarely seen on small craft, but when it does occur, it looks as though you are accompanied by a fleet of other vessels, all in a perfectly straight line and at equal distances from each other. Unless you've got caught up in a military exercise, such a thing is so unlikely that you probably won't be fooled by it!

There are one or two other bizarre effects which very occasionally occur. Overhead power cables, for instance, are usually far too thin to show up on radar in their own right, but they may be surrounded by a magnetic field which does. Unfortunately, the magnetic field only shows up where the radar beam is at right angles to the cable, so you don't see the whole cable at once. The effect, where a cable crosses a channel, is as though a singularly irritating little ferry is setting off to cross the channel as you approach. Whatever you do to avoid it, the ghost 'ferry' will appear to alter course or speed so as to cause a collision.

Side lobe echoes

Side lobe echoes, by contrast, are very common indeed. They are caused by stray beams of radar energy escaping from the radar scanner alongside the main beam.

They may be weak, by comparison with the main beam, but if they strike a good

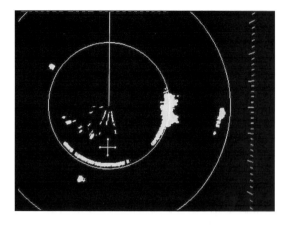

Another example of side lobe echoes, but this time the other vessel (right of centre) is so close that the echo bounces off our own vessel, and goes back for a second trip, producing the weaker double-echo visible on the extreme right.

reflector at short range, each of these side lobes can be enough to produce a contact on the screen. It will be at the same range as the real contact, but on a slightly different bearing, so side lobe echoes appear either as a curving string of contacts or as a crescent-shaped smear. The real contact is the biggest and strongest one, roughly in the middle of the string or smear.

Second trace echoes

Second trace echoes occur when an echo from some very distant object is received so late that the radar has already transmitted another pulse. The radar doesn't know that the late-returning echo came from the pulse before, so it produces a contact on the screen at a very much shorter range than the real object.

Radar manufacturers minimise the risk of second trace echoes by producing radars with relatively long pulse repetition intervals. Suppose, for instance, that your radar has a PRF of 750Hz, giving it a PRI of about 1333 microseconds.

Now suppose that the radar transmits a

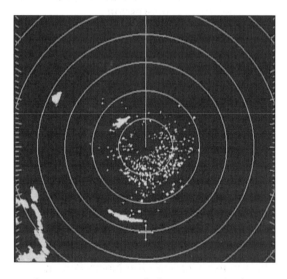

A ship crossing astern (below centre) is almost broadside-on, so it is producing strong side lobe echoes.

pulse which is reflected by a large target about 120 miles away. The returning pulse arrives back at the scanner 1483 microseconds after it was transmitted. Of course, while that pulse was in flight, the radar transmitted another pulse, 1333 microseconds after the first. It assumes that the echo was produced by the second pulse, rather than the first, so it produces a contact on the screen at a range of 12 miles rather than 120.

It should be pretty obvious from the huge ranges involved that second trace echoes aren't exactly common. In fact, so far as small craft are concerned, they are perhaps the rarest and most surprising of all the types of false echoes.

Weather effects

One of the main reasons for buying a radar must be its ability to 'see through fog', but it's important to be aware of the fact that weather conditions can still affect its performance. Rain – especially rain made up of very large drops such as you find falling from towering nimbocumulus behind a cold front – is quite capable of absorbing radar energy, and restricting the ability of the radar to detect targets in or beyond the rain. Hail, snow, and light rain have a much less serious effect, and fog or drizzle make almost no difference at all.

Other meteorological conditions can change the behaviour of radar waves, making them bend over the horizon rather more than usual, or straightening them out to reduce the distance to the radar horizon.

Sub-refraction

Sub-refraction reduces the extent to which the radar beam bends around the horizon, so it reduces the distance to the horizon, and reduces the range at which targets may become visible. Sub-refraction conditions occur when cold air passes over a relatively warm sea. They can also develop when the

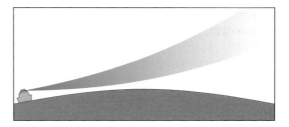

Fig 47 *Sub-refraction occurs when weather conditions distort the radar beam away from the surface of the Earth.*

Fig 48 *Super-refraction occurs when weather conditions encourage the radar beam to follow the curvature of the Earth.*

air at sea level is drier than the air a few metres above it, such as may happen in the warm sector of a depression.

Super-refraction

Super-refraction is the opposite in every respect; it expands the radar horizon, and happens when warm air lies over a cool sea, especially if the low-lying air is moister than the air above it or if the atmospheric pressure is high. Super-refractive conditions are present to some extent almost all the time at sea: that is why the radar horizon formula (page 100) puts the horizon slightly further away than the corresponding calculation for the visible horizon. In early summer, however, it's quite common for super-refraction to be more pronounced: in the English Channel, the North Sea, and the Mediterranean, one day in five is ripe for increased super-refraction to occur. Unfortunately, although super-refraction can make a little radar go a lot further, it's something of a mixed blessing because it greatly increases the amount of radar interference you're likely to experience.

A particularly extreme form of super-refraction is known as **ducting**, in which meteorological conditions create what is effectively a giant waveguide a few metres above the surface of the sea, enormously increasing the range of even a small radar. It's in these conditions that second trace echoes are most likely. Fortunately, per-haps, ducting conditions are very rare around the UK, though they do sometimes occur in the Mediterranean.

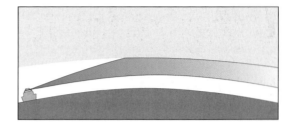

Fig 49 *Ducting occurs when weather condi-tions form a duct, trapping the radar beam close to the surface of the sea.*

14

Using radar for collision avoidance

Most yachtsmen and motor boaters probably invest in radar because of its unique ability to help avoid collisions. Such is its importance, in that respect, that it is the only electronic navigation aid to be specifically mentioned in the International Regulations for the Prevention of Collisions at Sea.

Radar and the Colregs

Rule 5

Every vessel shall at all times maintain a proper look-out by sight and hearing as well as by all available means appropriate to the prevailing circumstances and conditions so as to make a full appraisal of the situation and of the risk of collision.

> ▶▶ *This is one of the most fundamental rules of all, yet one of the most common causes of collisions is that the watchkeeper on one vessel simply didn't see the other until it was too late. The rule doesn't specifically mention radar, but it's pretty obvious that radar is covered by the catch-all phrase 'all available means'.*
>
> *This could be taken to mean that 'if you've got radar, you must use it', but it's not quite as dogmatic as that: if you don't have anyone on board capable of operating and understanding the radar, or if you need to preserve your power*

supplies, then you could sensibly argue that the radar is not 'available'. In daylight, clear visibility, and a moderate sea state, you could equally argue that it is not appropriate.

Rule 7

(a) Every vessel shall use all available means appropriate to the prevailing circumstances and conditions to determine if risk of collision exists. If there is any doubt such risk shall be deemed to exist.
(b) Proper use shall be made of radar equipment if fitted and operational, including long-range scanning to obtain early warning of risk of collision and radar plotting or equivalent systematic observation of detected objects.
(c) Assumptions shall not be made on the basis of scanty information, especially scanty radar information.
(d) In determining if risk of collision exists the following considerations shall be among those taken into account:
    (i) such risk shall be deemed to exist if the compass bearing of an approaching vessel does not appreciably change;
    (ii) such risk may sometimes exist even when an appreciable bearing change is evident, particularly when approaching a very large vessel or a tow or when approaching a vessel at close range.

▶▶ *This appears to start off simply by restating Rule 5, but it reinforces the importance of radar, and makes the point that 'proper use' of radar means more than having it switched on and being able to say 'Ooh look! There's a ship!'*

The phrase 'Long-range scanning' means different things to different people, but the intention is that you should be aware of the presence of other vessels as soon as possible, while there is still plenty of time to decide what you need to do about them. In practical terms, for most small craft, that probably means having your radar operating on a range scale of somewhere between 8 and 16 miles. There's not much point using a longer range than that, because the radar horizon makes it unlikely that you'll detect ships at much more than 10–15 miles.

'Radar plotting' means watching the behaviour of a contact on the screen, in order to assess the risk of collision and to work out the other vessel's course and

speed. It's impossible to overstress the importance of radar plotting, but we still hear of so-called 'radar assisted collisions' in which a pair of professional watchkeepers drive their ships into the headlines by running into each other. All too often, the subsequent enquiry reveals that it was because one of them relied on intuition, instead of taking the trouble to work out what was really happening.

Rule 19

(d) A vessel which detects by radar alone the presence of another vessel shall determine if a close-quarters situation is developing and/or risk of collision exists. If so, she shall take avoiding action in ample time, provided that when such action consists of an alteration in course, so far as possible the following shall be avoided:

(i) an alteration of course to port for a vessel forward of the beam, other than for a vessel being overtaken;

(ii) an alteration of course towards a vessel abeam or abaft the beam.

Plotting: sheets or screen?

Radar plotting involves a certain amount of simple geometry. It's no more complicated than that which is involved in traditional chart-work – in fact, it has a lot in common with working up an estimated position, or calculating a course to steer.

There are two possible ways of drawing the diagrams involved. One is to transfer the positions of contacts from the radar display to a plotting sheet – a paper representation of the radar screen. This is slightly tedious, and demands a supply of plotting sheets. On the other hand, it's accurate and leaves you with a record of what happened.

The alternative is to draw straight onto the radar screen itself, using either a white-board marker or a grease-pencil. This is quick, simple, and doesn't require special stationery. If your screen has an anti-reflective coating on it, there is a slight risk that you may damage the coating, but the main drawback is that the radar image is formed inside the screen and your plotting marks will be on the outside. The difference may only be a couple of millimetres, but it's enough to introduce parallax errors which affect the accuracy of your result. It's important, especially on a small screen, to try to make sure that you look at the screen from exactly the same direction every time you make a mark on it.

▶▶ Rule 19 applies to vessels which are not in sight of each other, in or near an area of restricted visibility, when it takes over from all the usual steering and sailing rules and imposes a simple 'slow down or stop if there's anything in front' rule in their place.

Paragraph 19(d), however, gives radar-equipped vessels the added responsibility of avoiding close-quarters situations altogether.

Yet again, it shows the importance of radar plotting, because unless you can tell whether the vessel ahead of you is being overtaken or whether you are crossing each other, you can't obey the rule!

Assessing the risk

Earlier, on page 93, we said that on a relative motion display, 'your own vessel is always at the centre of the picture'. This is one of the great strengths of a relative motion display, because it means that if a contact on the screen appears to be sliding straight towards the centre, you know that sooner or later, unless one of you does something about the situation, you and the approaching vessel will end up in the same place as each other!

One very quick and easy way of checking this is to put the electronic bearing line on the contact when it first appears. If, a few minutes later, the contact is still on the EBL but at closer range, then it's a threat.

If you are using a stabilised display (a north-up or course-up mode) then the EBL is the equivalent of a compass bearing: by sliding down the EBL, the contact shows that it is on a steady bearing, so it passes the tried and trusted test of a collision risk.

An unstabilised (head-up) display is slightly different. You can easily make the contact move away from the EBL simply by allowing the boat to wander a few degrees off course. That is why Rule 7(d)(i)

specifies a compass bearing rather than a relative bearing. Even so, the EBL test is still useful, because so long as you are holding a reasonably steady course it provides a quick and simple check – the radar equivalent of lining up an approaching ship with a guardrail to see whether the bearing seems to be changing.

Closest point of approach

The essence of the steady bearing test for assessing the risk of collision is that if a contact has been sliding down a straight line towards the centre of the screen for a few minutes, then unless someone does something about it, it will go on doing so.

Suppose, however, that it isn't aiming for the centre of the screen – that it's slipping, instead, along a straight line that passes half a mile from the centre.

The same principle holds good: unless someone does something to change the situation, the contact will keep on moving across the screen in the same direction, until it passes half a mile from the centre of the screen and then slides away on the other side.

If your radar has a facility known as a floating EBL (see page 97), it is a good idea to put the centre point of the EBL on the contact. A few minutes later, adjust the direction of the EBL – without moving its centre – so that it again passes through the contact. The EBL now represents the future movement of the contact across the screen.

An alternative, especially if you don't have a floating EBL, is to mark or plot the position of the contact when you first see it: mark or plot it again six minutes later, and again six minutes later still. Then, draw a straight line passing through all three positions, to represent the apparent movement of the contact across the screen, and extend it to represent the contact's likely future movement.

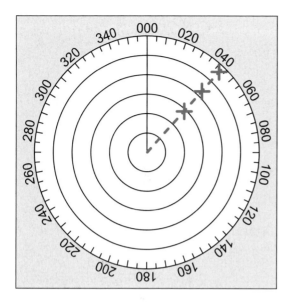

Fig 50 *A contact whose bearing does not appear to be changing will eventually reach the centre of the screen – which is where we are!*

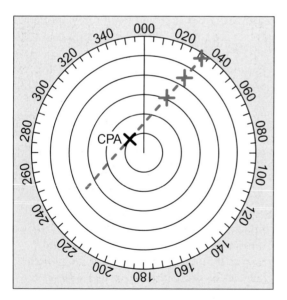

Fig 51 *A contact whose bearing is changing will probably miss us. By projecting its past movement onwards, it is possible to predict its closest point of approach.*

The closest point of approach (CPA) is the point on the line which is closest to the centre of the screen. It's easy to assume that the CPA will be when the other vessel is directly ahead or astern of you. That isn't necessarily true, though it can be useful to know, for instance, that a ship is going to pass two miles ahead.

The virtue of plotting at regular intervals is that it gives a good impression of how quickly the contact is moving across the screen. From this, you can easily go a stage further and estimate when the other vessel will cross ahead or astern of you, and when it will reach its CPA. This is often known as TCPA (Time to CPA).

What is an acceptable CPA?

As soon as you work out a CPA, it begs the question whether this is acceptable or whether it's a near miss.

To the masters of two large container ships meeting in mid ocean, a CPA of two or three miles might seem like a near miss. To the skippers of two racing yachts, jostling for position on a crowded start line, two or three metres might seem almost generous. The vast majority of incidents fall somewhere between these two extremes, depending on the size, speed, and manoevrability of the vessels concerned; whether it's a head-on, overtaking, or crossing situation; the weather conditions; whether it's daylight or night, and so on.

The point is that there are no hard and fast rules, so although the radar can provide the information, it is always up to the human watchkeeper or skipper to make the decision.

▶▶ If the contact (on the radar screen) seems set to cross your heading marker, the other vessel is likely to pass ahead of you, and you will cross behind it. This is generally safer than if the contact seems likely to pass behind you, implying that you will be cutting across the bows of the other vessel.

Finding course and speed

So far, our assessment of collision risk and of CPA has been based solely on the movement of blobs on the radar screen: we've been interested in whether one blob is going to share the centre of the screen with us, or whether it is going to miss it by half a mile or a mile or two.

It's often useful, though, to know more about the other vessel than just that there's a risk of hitting it! Knowing its course and speed enables us to plan better strategies for avoiding it.

The principle of relative motion

If we were stationary, on still water and making no way through the water, the problem would be simple. Stationary objects would appear as stationary contacts, and moving objects would appear to move on the radar screen in just the same way as they move in the real world. It's when we start moving that the problems begin.

Imagine, for instance, that there is a boat directly ahead of us, heading in the same direction but going much more slowly. As time passes, we would catch it up: its range, in other words, would reduce. On a head-up radar screen it would appear as a contact sliding down the heading mark towards the centre. It could very easily be mistaken for something coming straight towards us, rather than something that is running away from us.

Now let's think what would happen to the contact representing a stationary object, such as a buoy. If we start by aiming straight at it, then it, too, will appear to slide straight down the heading mark. If we are doing 6 knots, then after 6 minutes, its range will have reduced by 0.6 miles[6], so the speed at which the contact appears to

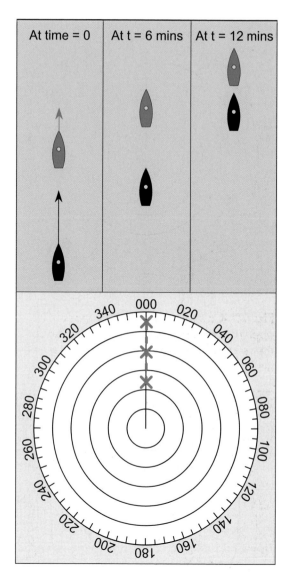

Fig 52 *A contact's movement on the radar screen is seldom the same as the target's movement through the water. Here, the contact 'coming towards us' on the radar screen is really a slower-moving vessel that we are overtaking.*

---

[6]It is very common, in radar plotting and high speed navigation, to refer to time intervals of 6, 12, 18, 24 minutes and so on. The reason for this is that 6 minutes is one tenth of an hour. It simplifies the arithmetic, because you can multiply or divide by ten simply by moving the decimal point. One tenth of 15.2 knots, for instance, is 1.52 knots, and ten times 0.80 miles is 8.0 miles.

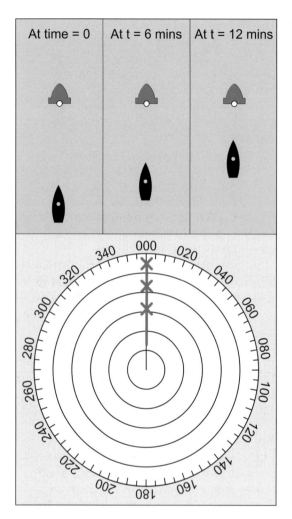

Fig 53 *The contact representing a stationary target, directly ahead, moves straight down the heading mark, at a speed equal to our own.*

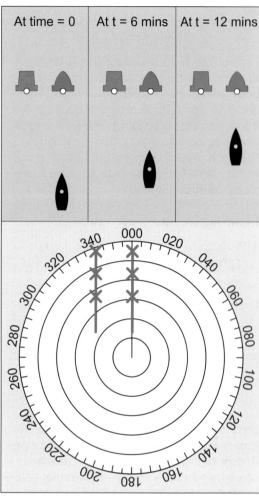

Fig 54 *The contact representing another stationary target moves parallel to the heading mark, at a speed equal to our own.*

move on the radar screen is exactly equal to our own speed, but it appears to be moving in the opposite direction.

Now imagine that the buoy in question is one of a pair, marking a mile-wide channel. As you aim straight for one of them, the other one will appear slightly off to one side. As you get closer and closer to the one that is directly ahead, the other one will also appear to move down your radar

screen towards its closest point of approach, a mile away and directly abeam.

By looking at the behaviour of this second buoy, we can deduce a set of simple rules about the behaviour of any contact that represents a stationary target:

- It moves parallel to the heading mark.

- It moves in the opposite direction to the heading mark.

- It moves at the same speed as our own movement through the water.

Strictly speaking these rules will be distorted by the effect of tides or currents, because our own vessel won't be moving in the direction indicated by the heading mark. For collision avoidance purposes, however, we can ignore this, and memorise these three rules parrot-fashion.

Now let's look again at a potential collision situation (Fig 55).

Plotting in head-up mode

- We are doing 25 knots, and a contact has appeared at a range of 5 miles, bearing about 330° (relative).

- Six minutes later, its range has reduced to 3.8 miles, but its bearing has altered very little – perhaps 1°.

- After 12 minutes, the range has reduced to 2.6 miles, and its bearing has altered by another 1°.

Drawing a straight line through these three positions suggests that the future movement of the contact is likely to bring it very close to us, at the centre of the screen, and that it will eventually pass close behind us. This, however, tells us nothing about its course and speed.

Suppose that it had dropped a large buoy just as we first plotted its position. For a moment, the ship and the buoy would be in the same place in the real world, and would therefore appear in the same place on our radar screen. While the ship moves on, however, the buoy is left behind, to follow the rules for a stationary object. Its contact, therefore, moves parallel to the heading marker, in the opposite direction, and at a speed equal to our own – in this case 25 knots.

As the Fig 56, after six minutes, the buoy would be on our screen at a range of 3.0 miles, bearing 308°(R). After 12 minutes

we'd have passed it, and it would be 2.5 miles away on a bearing of 284°(R).

That's what is happening on the screen. In the real world, however, the buoy is stationary, so any difference between the position of the buoy and the position of the ship must be due to the movement of the ship.

After 12 minutes, we can see that they are three miles apart. A quick bit of mental arithmetic shows that if the ship has covered three miles in 12 minutes, it must have covered 1.5 miles in 6 minutes, and is likely to do 15 miles in 60 minutes. Its speed, in other words, must be 15 knots.

We can also see that to get from where the buoy is to where the ship is, the ship must have moved in an 020°(R) direction.

Of course, in the real world, ships don't go round dropping large radar-reflective buoys whenever we want them to! The rules for stationary objects, however, mean that we can do without a real buoy, but can draw in the position of an imaginary buoy instead.

So what?

Had we been dealing with this situation without radar, we might have seen another vessel as a dim smudge in the distance. Over a period of time, we might have been able to deduce that it was getting closer, and that since its bearing wasn't changing very much, there was a risk of collision.

Using radar gives us more information. It shows us that the bearing is almost steady, but that the other vessel is most likely to pass close astern – or that we are about to cut across its bows!

Radar plotting has given us even more information, telling us that the other vessel's course is converging with our own at an angle of about 20°, and that its speed is 15 knots. To grasp the significance of that, it may be helpful to sketch a picture of a boat on the radar plotting sheet, in the right place and pointing in the right

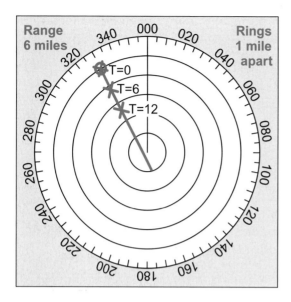

Fig 55 *This contact represents a threat. To decide what to do about it, it would be helpful to know its course and speed.*

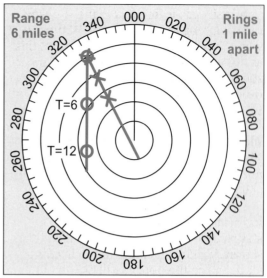

Fig 56 *The course and speed of a moving target can be calculated by comparing it with a stationary target.*

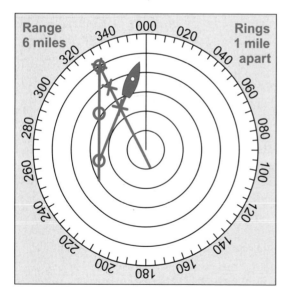

Fig 57 *The completed plot – in head-up mode.*

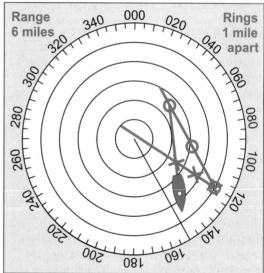

Fig 58 *The same situation, plotted in north-up mode.*

direction. Having done that, it becomes obvious that if this were a night-time encounter, we would be catching up on the other vessel, and that we would be in the arc covered by his white stern light. So far as the collision regulations are concerned, that means that we are an overtaking vessel, and must therefore give way.

It is situations like this that show why radar plotting is so important. Without it, it would have been too easy to interpret this as a crossing situation in which we are the stand-on vessel. Plotting reveals that it is an overtaking situation, in which it is up to us to give way.

North-up collision avoidance

The principles of collision avoidance in north-up mode are exactly the same using a head-up or course-up radar, but the geometry looks very different. The important thing is to remember that a stationary object doesn't move 'down' the screen: it moves 'parallel to the heading mark and in the opposite direction'.

Fig 58 shows the same example as Fig 57, but in north-up mode, and on a course of 150°.

Advanced radar plotting

For most recreational boat owners, and a fair number of professionals, being able to assess a target's CPA, TCPA, course and speed is enough, and the imaginary buoy technique is perfectly adequate. Others, however, may want to know more – to work out what will happen if you alter course, perhaps, or to calculate the course required to intercept a moving target. For these more advanced radar plotting jobs, it's sometimes useful to label the sides and corners of the vector triangle.

In classic radar plotting terminology, the first plot of the contact's position on the screen is labelled O, and its most recent position is labelled A. It may be easier to remember if you think that the line OA represents the Observed or Apparent movement of the other vessel.

The line representing the apparent movement of the imaginary buoy is based on the speed and direction of your own vessel. One end of it is already labelled O: the other end is labelled W so the line WO

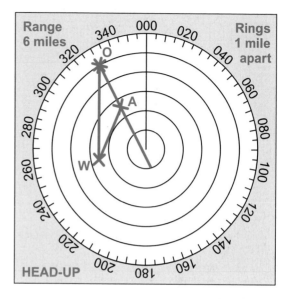

Fig 59 *Many people find it helpful to label the corners of the plotting triangle, using the standard letters O, W, and A.*

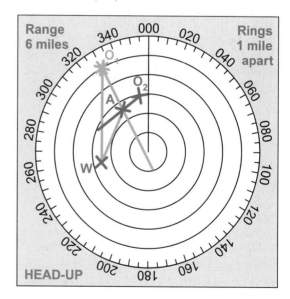

Fig 60 *From the same basic plot, it is possible to work out how the situation will change if we alter course or speed (see text).*

represents the Way of your Own vessel.

The third line, WA represents the Way of Another vessel – the target.

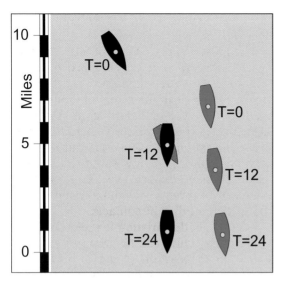

Fig 61 *A gull's eye view of the situation in Fig 60.*

The effect of altering course

Having established the other vessel's course and speed (WA) we could calculate how his relative movement would change if we altered course or speed, by leaving the WA that we've just calculated on the screen or plotting sheet, but drawing a new WO to correspond with our intended new course and speed.

In Fig 62, WO_1 represents our present course and speed: WO_2 represents a new course and speed, after we have slowed down to 20 knots and altered course 30° to starboard.

We can't change WA, because that is decided by the watchkeeper on the other vessel, but the fact that we now have a new WO_2 means that we also have a new AO_2, representing the Observed or Apparent movement of the contact after we have altered course. To find out how the situation will really look after we have altered our course and speed, we simply need to transfer the new AO_2 to the right bit of the screen, so that it starts from the present position of the contact.

Course to intercept

Most of us use radar to avoid collisions, but perhaps the most interesting of these advanced radar plotting techniques is used to calculate the course and speed required to deliberately create a close-quarters situation. The Police, Customs, and Navy, for

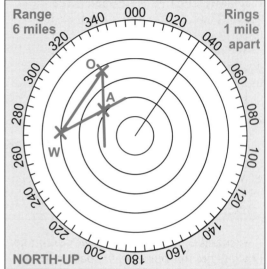

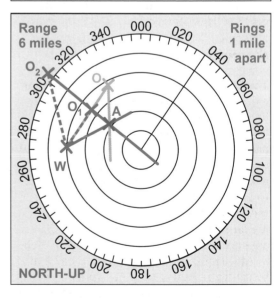

Fig 62 *For some purposes, it is useful to be able to set up a close-quarters situation deliberately (see text).*

instance, use this kind of technique to intercept another vessel.

The principle behind it is that we need to change the shape of the triangle so that OA points straight towards the centre of the screen. We can't move A, because that is the real contact. We can't change the length or direction of WA, either, because that is decided by the skipper of the other vessel. That, in turn, means that W is fixed.

We can, however, change our own course or speed to move O. There are usually many options.

Here, for instance:

- WO_1 shows that we could intercept by holding our present course and reducing speed by about 40%.

- WO_2 shows that we could also intercept by maintaining our present speed and altering 50° to port.

Remember that the longer we can make OA, the greater our closing speed will be, so the less time it will take to reach the point of interception.

Guard zones

The most fundamental purpose of radar in collision avoidance is to let us know that there is something else in our vicinity. Unfortunately, it can only do that if someone happens to be looking at the screen at the time – and in most boats, no-one is available or willing to devote 100% concentration to the radar. To overcome this, most radars incorporate a guard zone facility, which sounds an alarm whenever a contact appears in a designated area of the screen.

At its most basic, perhaps, a radar could be set up so that it sounded an alarm whenever any contact appeared, anywhere on the screen. In practice, however, this would be almost completely useless, because the alarm would be going off so

often that people would simply ignore it or switch it off.

The most common cause of false alarms is sea clutter, so all practical guard zones allow you to set up a minimum range so that contacts closer than the minimum distance don't trigger the alarm at all. By the same token, you may have your radar set to a 24-mile setting for navigation purposes, without wanting to know about ships that are more than 10 miles away. The guard zone can be given a maximum range so that it ignores distant contacts.

A more subtle variation is a sectored guard zone, which can be arranged to ignore contacts astern, ahead, or on the beam. This can be useful if, for instance, you are running parallel to a coastline, and don't want the alarm sounding continuously because the radar is detecting the land alongside you, or if you are following a traffic separation scheme and don't want to know about the vessels ahead or astern of you that are on parallel courses and at much the same speed.

The trouble with guard zones is that if you set one up so that it ignores all the possible false alarms, it can all too easily ignore the things that you want to know about as well. A particular problem is that a small vessel may easily creep in under your guard zone by not appearing on the screen until it is within the minimum range you have selected.

Overall, it's fair to say that a well set-up guard zone is better than not keeping a radar watch at all, but it is no substitute for a human operator keeping a regular eye on the radar screen.

ARPA and MARPA

An increasing number of modern radars have a facility known as an Automatic Radar Plotting Aid (ARPA). It does exactly what the name suggests: it monitors the apparent movement of contacts on the screen, and works out their courses, speeds, CPAs, and times to CPA.

Strictly speaking, in order to qualify for the name 'ARPA', the equipment has to meet some pretty stringent performance criteria laid down by the International Maritime Organisation, so for vessels which don't have to conform to IMO regulations[7], several companies offer less sophisticated versions known as EPA (Electronic Plotting Aid) or MARPA (Mini ARPA).

One fundamental difference between ARPA and MARPA is that ARPA monitors all the targets on the screen, and tests each one against a series of different criteria such as its size, and whether it shows up on every sweep. It then ignores very large contacts such as land, and intermittent contacts such as sea clutter, but carries on monitoring the position of all the others. MARPA, by contrast, misses out this 'automatic acquisition' facility, and relies on the operator using the cursor to highlight the contacts that he is interested in.

At first, the only effect of this is that the 'interesting' contact is marked, usually with a square box around it. Behind the scenes, however, the ARPA/MARPA software continues to monitor its movement until, after about a minute or so, it has gathered enough information to calculate the target's course, speed, CPA, and TCPA. At this point, the square box marker turns into a circle, and sprouts a 'vector' showing the contact's course and speed – the longer the vector line, the faster it is travelling. The same information, along with its CPA and TCPA, can also be shown in a data box elsewhere on the radar display.

If the CPA falls below some pre-set limit,

chosen by the operator, the circle marker will change again, usually to a triangle, and may flash or change colour to draw attention to the fact that the ARPA/MARPA has identified it as 'dangerous'. Similarly, it will change to another shape, such as a diamond, if the radar fails to detect the target for six consecutive sweeps of its scanner.

ARPA and MARPA are clever devices that can calculate courses, speeds, and collision risks in a fraction of the time that it would take a human, but they are not infallible. In particular, the information that they can provide is only as good as the data they receive from the log, compass, and radar, and they will only do what you tell them to: if you have asked for relative courses and speeds, that is exactly what they will show you – rather than the true courses and speeds you may have been expecting.

▶▶ Read the manual !

Bear in mind, too, that ARPA and MARPA will have difficulty tracking a target which keeps appearing and disappearing, or which jumps around the screen, so it needs to be used with caution when:

- The contact is weak or intermittent.

- The contact is close to other contacts or land.

- You or the target vessel are altering course or speed.

- The sea is rough enough to produce a lot of sea clutter or for the contact to be lost in deep troughs.

[7]IMO regulations distinguish between Electronic Plotting Aids (EPA), Automatic Tracking Aids (ATA) and ARPA, with different capabilities and performance standards. They also set different carriage requirements for vessels of different sizes, ranging from one EPA for ships of less than 500 tons to an ARPA and an ATA for those over 10,000 tons. Small craft, yachts, and ships of less than 300 tons are exempt.

15

Using radar for navigation and pilotage

Anyone brought up on traditional navigation techniques is likely to spot at least one way in which radar can be used to fix your boat's position.

Fix by radar bearings

The classic three-point visual fix is based on the idea that if you take a bearing of a landmark by looking across the top of a compass towards it, then your line of sight can be represented on the chart by a pencil line drawn along that bearing and passing through the landmark. Your position must be somewhere along that line, so it's called a position line.

Doing the same thing with another land-mark produces a second position line. There is only one place that you can possibly be if you are on two different position lines at once, and that is where they cross. If everything in a navigator's life were 100% reliable and perfectly accurate, then two intersecting position lines would be enough for a fix. In real life, however, things are never quite that simple, so it is better to take a third bearing. The third bearing does not necessarily make a fix more accurate, but it does make it more reliable, by guarding against gross errors such as a landmark wrongly identified or a bearing wrongly read or plotted.

In theory, you'd expect all three position lines to cross at a single point, with each one confirming the accuracy of the other two. Such perfect fixes happen so rarely in real life that they are grounds for suspicion rather than congratulation. More often, the three lines intersect to form a triangle that is still named after a piece of impractical 18th-century headgear – a cocked hat.

Although it's often said that 'you must be somewhere inside the cocked hat', that isn't true. Statistical theory actually suggests that there is only a 25% chance of being inside the cocked hat, so there's a 75% chance of being outside it! Nevertheless, you can be a lot more confident about the position indicated by a nice, neat, compact cocked hat than by one that straggles around all over the chart.

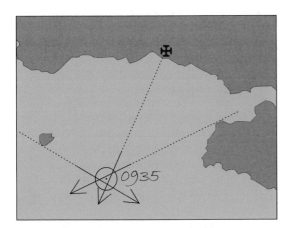

Fig 63 A classic three-point fix by visual bearings.

When taking a fix by visual bearings, there are several things you can do to minimise the size of the cocked hat and increase the accuracy of the resulting fix:

• Identify your marks.

• Choose marks that are well spread.

• Choose near marks rather than distant ones.

• Take bearings quickly, but accurately.

• Take the bearing which is changing quickest, last.

The first, and most obvious, is to make sure that the landmarks are correctly identified. It is utterly pointless to take a bearing of something that isn't on the chart, or to try to take a bearing of something that is on the chart but which you can't actually see. Neither is there much merit in having an accurate bearing of something like a church spire when the chart shows that it could be any of three or four different churches.

Headlands often make good landmarks: they are often easy to see, easy to identify, and are clearly charted. Even so, they need to be chosen with some care. Cliffs, dropping almost vertically into deep water, are fine. Gently sloping headlands, however, can be misleading. The chart, inevitably, shows a definite, hard edge between land and sea. In real life, of course, that isn't the case, and the high tide mark may be in a very different place from the water's edge at low tide. If you are more than a couple of miles away, you may not even be seeing the edge of the land at all, because it could be below the horizon.

The effect of bearing errors can be minimised by choosing your landmarks carefully. Ideally, they should be spread around the horizon, so that the position lines gross as the largest possible angle. For a fix using two position lines, the optimum angle between the position lines is 90°. For

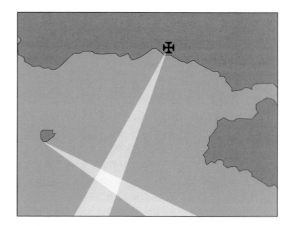

Fig 64 *The possibility of errors in the measured bearings produces a 'diamond of uncertainty'. It is generally small if the bearings intersect at a large angle.*

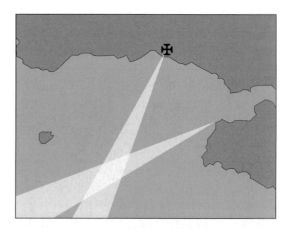

Fig 65 *The diamond of uncertainty is much bigger if the bearings intersect at a shallow angle.*

three position lines, it is either 60° or 120°.

Close objects are better than distant ones, even if the distant ones are more conspicuous. It's pretty self-evident why that should be so, if you imagine yourself passing a small object such as a buoy or a beacon tower. If you aim to leave it 100m to port, then in the space of 200m its bearing will change by 90°. On average, then, 1°

of bearing change corresponds to about 2m of movement. Now imagine that you are passing the same mark, at a distance of half a mile (≃ 1000m). To achieve the same 90° change in bearing, you need to move 2000m, so each degree of bearing change now corresponds to 20m instead of 2m.

The speed and order in which you take bearings can make a difference, too, especially on a fast-moving boat. Suppose, for instance, that it takes three minutes to take and plot a fix, and that you are moving at 20 knots. The boat will move a mile while you are busily working out where it was! To minimise this, bearings need to be taken as quickly as possible and in the right order. Bearings directly ahead or astern generally change relatively slowly compared with those directly abeam, so it is less important if they are slightly out of date. The general rule of thumb is that bearings which are

VRM/EBL 1
BRG 142° T
RNG 2.326nm

Most modern radars use a cursor to control the variable range marker and electronic bearing line simultaneously.

changing quickly should be taken last.

The principle of a fix by radar bearings is exactly the same as a fix by visual bearings, and exactly the same five points apply. The way the rules are applied, however, is slightly different.

Radar can't pick out a church from a block of flats or a row of houses. This means that many visual landmarks are useless for radar fixing. On the other hand, it is often almost impossible, with the naked eye, to pick out a jetty or promontory that is sticking out from the coastline, and pointing straight towards you. On radar, however, such things stand out like sore thumbs!

Be particularly wary of sloping headlands. The fact that radar can 'see' clearly through fog and haze makes it tempting to take bearings of headlands that are out of sight. Look carefully at the contour lines on the chart to make sure that you're not taking a bearing of something which could be dropping below the horizon or of a shoreline that moves as the tide rises and falls.

In the case of a visual fix, the argument in favour of near objects was a matter of simple geometry. In a radar fix, however, there are other factors to consider, such as the fact that you can take a bearing more accurately if the landmark in question is near the edge of the screen on a short range setting than if it is near the middle on a much longer range setting. Go for near objects, with the radar on the shortest range scale you can.

Finally, remember that taking bearings is not radar's strong point. Even a carefully-installed north-up radar is subject to various errors, such as the effect of beamwidth; the possibility that its heading mark is not perfectly lined up with the boat; compass error; operator error; and straightforward mathematical mistakes. To these, on a head-up radar, must be added the far greater risk of helmsman error and the fact that the extra step in the bearing calculation (see page 97) increases the chances of a mistake.

Although we've seen that radar bearings can be used for navigation, they aren't the first choice method.

Fix by radar ranges

The principles of a fix by radar ranges are uncannily similar to those of a fix by visual or radar bearings.

Suppose, for instance, that you measure the range to a landmark as three miles. If it is three miles from you, then obviously you must also be three miles from it. In other words, you must be somewhere on the circumference of a circle whose radius is three miles and whose centre is at the land-mark. The circle is a position line, very much like the straight position line formed by a visual bearing.

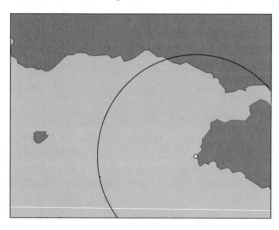

Fig 66 *Measuring the range of a landmark produces a circular position line.*

If you repeat the process, measuring the range of a second landmark, you'll get a second position line. As in the case of a fix by visual bearings, the only place you can be on both position lines at once is where they cross. A slight snag is that two circles will either not meet at all, or will intersect

each other twice. If they don't meet at all, then there is something badly wrong with your fix! If they intersect twice you will have two possible positions. In most cases, one of the two is clearly wrong. In the remaining minority of cases, the ambiguity is most easily sorted out by using a third position line. In practice, even when you have an unambiguous fix from two position lines, it is still best to add a third one, as a cross check on the other two.

The same five rules apply to a fix by radar ranges.

The point about near objects is still true for a radar range fix, but for a different reason than applies to a visual bearing fix. Partly, it is to do with the size of the image on the radar screen: it is simply easier to position the VRM accurately on a short range setting than on a longer one. It's also worth remembering, though, that long ranges use longer pulse lengths, so the radar's range discrimination is reduced at longer ranges.

The 'changing quickly' point also warrants a bit more explanation, because so many old-school navigators have learned the rule in the form 'take bearings ahead or astern first'. In the case of ranges, that

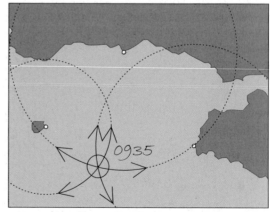

Fig 67 *Three intersecting range circles produce a reliable fix, with small errors and no arithmetic.*

needs to be reversed: the range of something changes most quickly when you are heading straight towards it or away from it, and most slowly as you pass it. Measure the range of objects which are abeam, first.

Plotting a range fix poses very few problems: assuming your radar has been properly set up, there is no need to do any calculation at all. Plotting each range is a simple matter of opening a pair of drawing compasses to the right distance, sticking the point in the chart at the landmark you took the range from, and making an arc with the pencil end of the compass.

Range error

Radar is generally very good at measuring ranges. One possible source of error, however, is known as 'display timing' or 'index' error, and arises if the receiver thinks the pulse was transmitted slightly earlier or later than it really was. It produces a fairly small but constant error. Because it's constant, it is most noticeable on short ranges: an index error of 50m may be obvious if you are operating on a range scale of half a mile, but

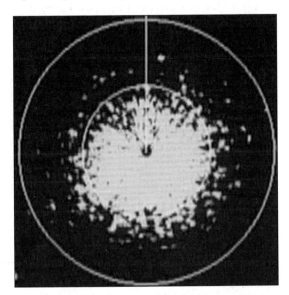

The 'black hole' in the centre of this screen suggests that there may be a timing error.

will probably pass unnoticed at 20 miles.

The definitive check for timing error is to put the boat close to a straight-sided target such as a bridge or harbour wall, which should produce a straight-sided contact. If the display timing is wrong, however, the nearest part of the contact may look as though it is being pulled towards the centre of the screen, or pushed away from it. If this is the case, it is worth checking with the manufacturers' handbook: in many modern radars, display timing is a simple adjustment that is easily corrected through the 'set-up' menu.

An alternative, less reliable test, is to switch the radar to its shortest range scale and look at the bright blob in the centre of the screen. If it has a dark hole in its centre, then the radar will measure ranges as being slightly longer than they really are, by a distance equal to the radius of the dark spot. This method has the advantage that it doesn't need a bridge or wall: on the other hand, it can't tell you if the radar is understating ranges.

A third method is to steer roughly midway between two fixed and charted objects, and measure the distance of each one as you pass between them. If you add these two ranges together, they should add up to the total distance between the two objects, which you can measure on the chart. If they do not, then you can either try to correct the timing error through the radar's set-up menu, or you can halve the discrepancy between the measured distance and the charted distance, and apply that figure as a correction to all your measured ranges.

Mixed fixes

There's no reason why all the position lines that make up a fix should come from the same source. It's often better, in fact, to use a mixture of position lines, and to combine a visual transit with a compass bearing and a radar range, for instance, so long as you follow the five general rules for each position line.

A special case arises when you have only one landmark available. This situation makes it particularly tempting to use a range and bearing of the same object, both measured by radar. The result, on the chart, invariably looks good: the range-based position line always cuts the bearing position line at 90°, to give a reassuringly precise-looking fix. It may be every bit as good as it looks. The trouble is that if you have wrongly identified the landmark – if you've taken the range and bearing of a drifting fishing boat, for instance, instead of the beacon tower that you thought you were looking at – then the whole fix will be wrong, but with nothing to warn you of the fact. It is much better, in this situation, to use a visual bearing crossed with a radar range. Not only is each method being used for what it is best at, but it also encourages you to look at what you're using as a landmark.

Pilotage

Radar's ability to 'see' through fog or darkness, to measure distances to an accuracy of metres, and to show the real world rather than the traffic-free version portrayed on charts, makes it a particularly powerful pilotage tool.

Just as in visual pilotage, the object of radar pilotage is to navigate accurately along a pre-planned track through confined waters in which the business of taking and plotting fixes is impractical. There are several useful techniques, including clearing ranges (page 127) and parallel indexing (page 128), adopted from big-ship practice.

For small craft, however, there's another, simpler and more intuitive method which may be all that is required and which could, for want of a formal title, be called 'video gaming'.

Video game pilotage

The principle of video game pilotage is rather like 'eyeball' navigation, in which you pick a feature to aim for, such as a buoy, a gap between two islands, or simply choose the nearest bit of clear water, and aim for it.

In the case of blind pilotage by radar, of course, this means identifying your target on the screen, and altering course until the heading mark is pointing straight at it.

Using a head-up radar, the principle can be adapted slightly, in order to pass a set distance off a headland, for instance, by using a grease pencil or whiteboard marker to draw a line on the screen parallel to the heading marker, and the right distance away from it. Then it is simply a matter of steering the boat so as to keep the headland sliding along the marked line.

Video gaming is a perfectly reasonable technique for passing through a clearly-defined gap or following a well-marked channel, but it suffers the same drawbacks as eyeball navigation if there is any wind or tidal stream pushing the boat sideways, or if the line of the channel can't be easily

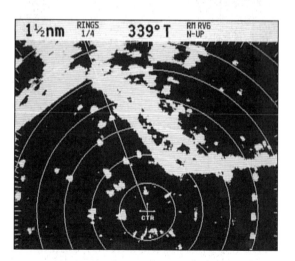

In a well-marked channel, and with little wind or tide, radar pilotage may be a simple matter of aiming the heading mark at the next buoy.

identified from the radar picture. It would be fine, for instance, for getting you through a rocky harbour entrance with sheer sides and no hazards in the middle, but it would be risky where the sea and river meet, and the river drops its cargo of silt to produce underwater mudflats, sticking out way beyond the visible shoreline.

Clearing ranges

A slightly more formal technique is known as clearing ranges. The principle is exactly the same as the clearing bearings used in visual pilotage, in which you note, from the chart, what the bearing of some conspicuous object would be if you were right on the edge of the safe water. By comparing the actual bearing with the measured bearing, you can tell at a glance whether you are on the 'safe' side of the clearing line or not.

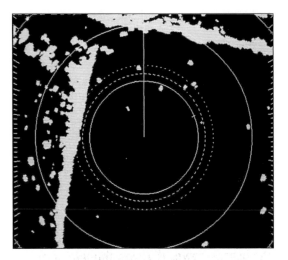

Using two VRMs, the clearing ranges can be shown on the radar screen. Using ranges, rather than bearings, means that this technique can be used on head-up radars.

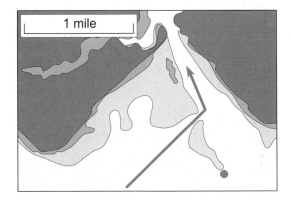

Fig 68 *Clearing ranges can be used to find safe water between invisible hazards.*

Clearing ranges are even easier. Suppose, for instance, that we're approaching the harbour entrance shown in Fig 68, from the west. A string of sandbanks extend southeastwards from the entrance, between us and the deep-water channel. Fortunately, there are smaller channels between the sandbanks.

From the chart, we can see that so long as we stay at least 0.6 miles from the shore, we cannot possibly hit the sandbanks to the north of our intended approach...and so long as we are within 0.7 miles of the shore, we will clear the sandbanks to the south.

Picking our way through the gap, then, becomes a simple matter of setting up VRMs on the radar screen at the relevant distances, and steering the boat to keep the shore sliding past between the two VRMs.

The important thing to appreciate about a clearing range is that it is rather like a handrail: if you are going to use it to support your navigation, you must make sure you have a secure hold of it before you need to rely on it.

Suppose, for instance, that you're approaching the Solent from Poole, and are intending to take the safe North channel, rather than the notorious Needles channel (Fig 69). A radar clearing range of Not Less than 0.4 miles off the mainland coast would keep you well clear of the Shingles Bank.

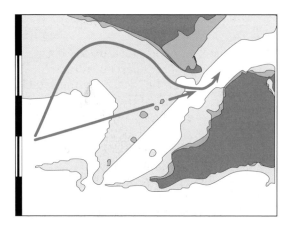

Fig 69 *There is a world of difference between 'keeping 0.4 miles off the coast' and 'aiming for a point 0.4 miles off the coast'.*

Notice, though, that this is not the same as saying 'aim for a point 0.4 miles off the coast', because if you were to do that, you could well run straight into the very hazard you were trying to avoid!

Parallel indexing

If you have access to a good north-up radar, the door is open to another, even more powerful pilotage tool known as parallel indexing.

The principle of parallel indexing is simple; it relies on the fact that if you are using a stabilised radar you can predict exactly where a fixed object will appear on the screen, and how it will appear to move across the screen.

Suppose, for instance, that we are intending to follow a northwesterly track,

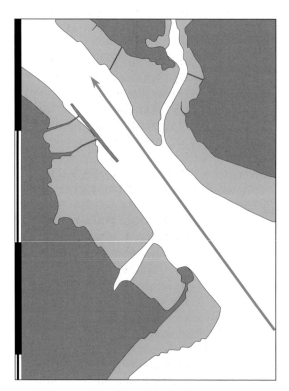

Fig 70 *A north-up radar can use parallel indexing. Here, the planned track passes 0.25 miles east of the jetty.*

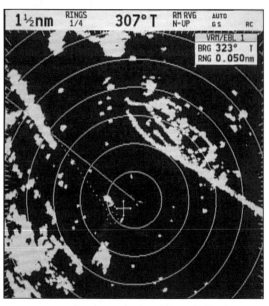

By setting up a floating EBL, so that it is in the same direction as our planned track, and 0.25 miles west of it, we can predict how the jetty should appear to move on the radar screen. In this case, the heading mark shows that we are having to steer well to port of our intended track to counteract a strong east-going tidal stream, to keep the jetty sliding along the EBL.

passing 0.25 miles east of the end of a conspicuous jetty. It is reasonably easy to see that so long as we really are on the planned track, the jetty will, at some stage, be a quarter of a mile to the west of us, and if we are moving from north-west, the contact representing the end of the jetty must appear to move in the opposite direction – south-east. We can represent its predicted movement either by using a floating EBL, or by drawing it onto the face of the screen with a white-board marker.

▶▶ If you don't fancy drawing on the screen of your radar, use a piece of thin acrylic sheet, sold for making overhead projector transparencies, to cover the screen, and draw on that.

When the time comes to actually make the passage, it is easy to see when we are on track, because the tip of the jetty will be just touching the planned line on the screen. So long as we stay on track, it must continue to move along the line. Not only that, but if we stray too far away from the jetty, the contact representing the jetty will drift away from the line and away from the centre of the screen. Staying on track, therefore, becomes a matter of steering the screen so that the line is always just touching the reference contact.

The whole thing, of course, stands or falls on whether you can predict the apparent movement of the reference contact accurately, and whether you can identify it correctly when you come to use it.

It is absolutely essential that the reference target is visible, identifiable, and unambiguous. There is no point, for instance, trying to use a buoy if it is too far away to be visible, or if it is surrounded by other boats.

The classic single-line index
Having selected your reference target, there are two ways of predicting its movement.

The first might be called the 'classic' method:
1 Draw your planned track on the chart, and highlight your reference target.
2 Draw a line parallel to the planned track, brushing the edge of the reference target.
3 Measure the distance between the two lines.
4 On the radar, set the VRM to the distance you measured in step 3.
5 Draw a line, just brushing the VRM, in the direction of your planned track.
6 Double check that if the reference target is supposed to pass your starboard side, that you have drawn the parallel index line on the starboard side, and vice versa.

The 'waypoint' index
An alternative, which dovetails rather neatly with the use of GPS as a pilotage tool, is to refer to the waypoints at each bend in your planned track:
1 Draw your planned track on the chart, and highlight your reference target.
2 Measure the range and bearing of your reference target from the first waypoint.
3 Measure the range and bearing of your reference target from the second waypoint.
4 Use the VRM and EBL to mark the corresponding ranges and bearings on the radar screen.
5 Join the two points that you have marked on the screen, with a straight line.
6 Double check that if the reference target is supposed to pass your starboard side, that you have drawn the parallel index line on the starboard side, and vice versa.

Multiple index lines
Many harbour entrances, in particular, involve more than following a single, straight-line track: you may have to alter course several times to follow a dog-leg channel. It makes very little difference to the principle of parallel indexing: the idea is still to predict how the contact would

move if you were on track, and then steer the boat so as to make the real contact follow the line you have drawn out for it on the screen. The only difference is that if your planned track on the chart has bends in it, the parallel index line on the screen will have bends in it, too.

It doesn't really matter which technique you use to construct the multiple lines, either, though the 'waypoint' technique is probably quicker.

▶▶ As a check, turn the chart upside down, so that it is in 'south-up' mode, and compare the shape of your intended track on the chart with the parallel index lines drawn on the radar screen: they should match!

Health warning
Parallel indexing is an incredibly powerful tool, and like most powerful tools, it can be dangerous in the wrong hands or when it is misapplied. Naval ships use it, as a matter of course, whenever they are entering or leaving harbour, regardless of the visibility, so that if they ever have to rely on it, it is simply a matter of dropping into a standard, well-practised routine. Even then, it is backed up by clearing ranges and occasional fixes when the opportunity arises.

▶▶ Parallel indexing breaks two cardinal rules:
- It relies on radar ranges and bearings from a single source with no cross checking.
- It relies on radar bearings, prone to error.

If a yacht's skipper is the only competent navigator and the only radar operator on board, he will almost certainly find that blind pilotage by parallel indexing is a high-risk, high-stress strategy. It really calls for at least two competent, well-practised people working as a team to achieve its potential.

Index

accuracy 8
  GPS 30-1
advanced radar plotting 117
alarms 35
altitude GPS 7
analogue displays 17
analogue sounders 65-6
antenna, radar 82-4
ARCS charts 50
ARPA 119
ASCII code 22
Automatic Radar Plotting Aid
  (ARPA) 119-20

basic displays 35
beamwidth, radar 82
bearing to waypoint 37
blind arcs 99
brilliance and contrast 88
built-in PCs 61

calibrating a log 74-5
calibration tips, compass 78
cathode ray tubes (CRTs) 18-19
central processing unit 12
changing charts 50
chart plotters 48-60
circle of error probability 10
clearing bearings 46-7
clearing ranges 127-8
closest point of approach (CPA)
  112
collision avoidance using radar
  109-120
collision regulations 109-11
compass rose, range and bearing 42
compasses 76-8
  calibration tips 78
  installation 77
  self-correction 77
cone strategy 43-4
controls 13
corridor strategy 44
course to steer by 59
course-up display 95
cross track error 38, 40
cross track error ladder 43
cursor control keys 14
cursor, radar 98

data 13
decluttering 53-4
differential GPS (DGPS) 31-3
digital displays 17
digital echo sounders 67-8
dilution of precision 9
direction 35
display, radar 85
displays 17
displays and controls 63
distance to waypoint 37
ducting 108

Earth,shape of 4
ECDIS (Electronic Chart Display
  and Information System) 48
echo sounders 65-71
  calibrating 71
  digital 67-8
  forward-looking 68-9
  installing 69
echoes, radar 105-7
electromagnetic logs 73
Electronic Charting System (ECS)
  48
electronic compasses 76-8
error 7, 8
  GPS 30
European Datum ED50 6
European Geostationary
  Navigational Overlay System
  (EGNOS) 32
European Terrestrial Reference
  System 6

false echoes 66,105
faults 8
finding course and speed 113
firmware 12
fish-finders 18, 66-7, 68
fix by radar bearings 121-3
fix by radar ranges 124-5
fix, plotting 41
fixing, two-dimensional 28
fluxgate compasses 76-8

gain 88
Galileo 33
Glonass 33
'go to' 37

GPS 26-47
  altitude 7
  pilotage 45
  satellites 28
  time 27
graphic displays 18
GRIB files 59-60
gridded binary files 59-60
guard zones, radar 119

hardware 12-25, 49
head-up display 93
horizontal datums 6

impeller, cleaning 74
initialising 34
interfacing, rules of 25
interference rejection 92-3
inverters 63

joystick 15

Kishmul of Ayr 2

laptops 61
latitude 5
lay lines 45
lens reflectors, radar 103
light emitting diodes (LEDs) 18
liquid crystal displays (LCDs) 19-20
log installing 73-4
logs 72-8
  electromagnetic 73
  pitot 72
longitude 5

machine/machine interface 21
MARPA 119-20
measuring error 10
measuring tools, radar 95-8
memory 12
menus 16
Mini ARPA 119-20
mixed fixes, radar 125-6
monitoring position by waypoint
  41
motherboard 12
mouse 14, 15
MTSAT Satellite-based
  Augmentation System (MSAS) 32

multifunction buttons 13-14
multipath errors 30-1

Nedlloyd Vespucci 3
NMEA 0183 code 22-5
north-up collision avoidance 117
north-up display 93-4

OBOJ systems 13
off-centring 95
opto-isolation 25
Ordnance Survey 6
overlays 57-60

parallel indexing 129-30
parallel port 22
passage plan 37
passage planning on a plotter 54
PC serial ports 21-2
pilotage 45, 126-30
pitot logs 72
plotting a fix 41
plotting in head-up mode 115
plotting position 7
plotting, radar 110
pointing tools 14
ports 12
position 35
    time and date 36
power consumption and safety for
    radar 86
power supplies 62
precision 9
pulse length frequency (PRF), radar
    81
pulse length, radar, 81

racons 104
radar 79-130
    avoidance using radar 109-120
    blind arcs 99
    brilliance and contrast 88
    closest point of approach (CPA)
        112
    collision risk assessment 111
    components 80
    course-up 95
    cross section 103
    cursor 98
    ducting 108
    finding course and speed 113
    fix 9,121-3,125-6
    gain 88
    guard zones 119
    head-up 93
    horizon 99-100
    improving the picture 90-3
    interference rejection 92-3

lens reflectors 103
measuring bearing 79
measuring range 79
measuring tools 95-8
north-up 93-4
north-up collision avoidance 117
off-centring 95
on-off and transmit-standby 87
pilotage 126-30
plotting 110
plotting in head-up mode 115
plotting, advanced 117-19
pulse length 81
rain clutter 91
range 89, 124-5
reflectors 102-3
reflectors, stacked arrays 103
sea clutter 90-1
shadow sectors 99
stabilisation 93-5
sub-refraction 107
super refraction 107
switching on 87
target enhancers (RTEs) 105
transmitter 80-2
transponders 104
true motion 95
tuning 89
variable range marker (VRM) 97
weather effects 107
what shows up 101-2
radial scan CRT 19
rain clutter 91-2
random errors 8
range 89
    and bearing of a compass rose
        42
    and bearing of waypoint 42
    error, radar 125
raster charts 49
raster CRT 19
receiver noise 31
receiver, radar 84
reflective displays 20
relative motion principle 113
repeatability 8
risk assessment, collision 111
rolling road display 40,57
route navigation 38-9
route summary 57
routes on a plotter 56-7
routes under way 39-41

Safety of Life at Sea (SOLAS) 48
SARTs 105
satellite codes 28-9
satellite differential GPS 32
satellites 28

sea clutter 90-1
second trace echoes 106
selective availability 29
serial ports 21-2, 22
set-up options 34-5
set-up procedure radar 90
shadow sectors 99
side lobes 84
    echoes 106
soft keys 16
software 12-25, 49
sonic logs 73
speed and direction 36-7
spiders web 42
starting error 39
sub-refraction, radar 107
super-refraction 107
switching on radar 87
systematic errors 8

thin film transistors (TFTs) 20
tidal streams 58
time and date 35
time to go 37
touch screens 15
TR cell 84-5
track pads 15
tracker ball 15
transducers 65, 69-71
transflective displays 20
transmissive displays 20
true motion 95
two-dimensional fixing 28

units 35
upwind sailing 43-5

variable range marker (VRM) 97
vector charts 50-4

Wahkuna 3
waypoint 46
    arrival 40-1
    navigation 37-8
    on a plotter 54-5
    range and position 42
    tips 46
    web 42
    to monitor position 41
    under way 39-41
weather information 59
WGS84 6
Wide Area Augmentation System
    (WAAS) 32

XTE limit 47

zoom in and out controls 53